11/06

WITHDR

31472 70135 2845

Morphine

DRUGS The Straight Facts

■ DRUGS
The Straight Facts

Morphine

Gregory D. Busse

Consulting Editor

David J. Triggle

University Professor
School of Pharmacy and Pharmaceutical Sciences
State University of New York at Buffalo

CHELSEA HOUSE
P U B L I S H E R S
An imprint of Infobase Publishing

Morphine

Chelsea House
An imprint of Infobase Publishing
132 West 31st Street
New York NY 10001

Library of Congress Cataloging-in-Publication Data

Busse, Gregory D.
    Morphine/Gregory D. Busse.
        p. cm.—(Drugs, the straight facts)
    Includes bibliographical references.
    ISBN 0-7910-8551-1
    1. Morphine—Juvenile literature. 2. Opium—Juvenile literature. I. Title.
II. Series.
RM666.M8B87 2005
362.29'3—DC22   2005 021242

Chelsea House books are available at special discounts when purchased in bulk quantities for businesses, associations, institutions, or sales promotions. Please call our Special Sales Department in New York at (212) 967-8800 or (800) 322-8755.

You can find Chelsea House on the World Wide Web at http://www.chelseahouse.com

Text and cover design by Terry Mallon

Printed in the United States of America

Bang 21C 10 9 8 7 6 5 4 3 2 1

This book is printed on acid-free paper.

All links and web addresses were checked and verified to be correct at the time of publication. Because of the dynamic nature of the web, some addresses and links may have changed since publication and may no longer be valid.

Table of Contents

The Use and Abuse of Drugs

The issues associated with drug use and abuse in contemporary society are vexing subjects, fraught with political agendas and ideals that often obscure essential information that teens need to know to have intelligent discussions about how to best deal with the problems associated with drug use and abuse. *Drugs: The Straight Facts* aims to provide this essential information through straightforward explanations of how an individual drug or group of drugs works in both therapeutic and non-therapeutic conditions; with historical information about the use and abuse of specific drugs; with discussion of drug policies in the United States; and with an ample list of further reading.

From the start, the series uses the word *"drug"* to describe psychoactive substances that are used for medicinal or non-medicinal purposes. Included in this broad category are substances that are legal or illegal. It is worth noting that humans have used many of these substances for hundreds, if not thousands of years. For example, traces of marijuana and cocaine have been found in Egyptian mummies; the use of peyote and Amanita fungi has long been a component of religious ceremonies worldwide; and alcohol production and consumption have been an integral part of many human cultures' social and religious ceremonies. One can speculate about why early human societies chose to use such drugs. Perhaps, anything that could provide relief from the harshness of life—anything that could make the poor conditions and fatigue associated with hard work easier to bear—was considered a welcome tonic. Life was likely to be, according to the 17th century English philosopher Thomas Hobbes, *"poor, nasty, brutish and short."* One can also speculate about modern human societies' continued use and abuse of drugs. Whatever the reasons, the consequences of sustained drug use are not insignificant—addiction, overdose, incarceration, and drug wars—and must be dealt with by an informed citizenry.

The problem that faces our society today is how to break the connection between our demand for illegal drugs and the willingness of largely outside countries to supply this highly profitable trade. This is the same problem we have faced since narcotics and cocaine were outlawed by the Harrison Narcotic Act of 1914, and we have yet to defeat it despite current expenditures of approximately $20 billion per year on "the war on drugs." The first step in meeting any challenge is always an intelligent and informed citizenry. The purpose of this series is to educate our readers so that they can make informed decisions about issues related to drugs and drug abuse.

SUGGESTED ADDITIONAL READING

David T. Courtwright, *Forces of Habit. Drugs and the Making of the Modern World.* Cambridge, Mass.: Harvard University Press, 2001. David Courtwright is Professor of History at the University of North Florida.

Richard Davenport-Hines, *The Pursuit of Oblivion. A Global History of Narcotics.* New York: Norton, 2002. The author is a professional historian and a member of the Royal Historical Society.

Aldous Huxley, *Brave New World.* New York: Harper & Row, 1932. Huxley's book, written in 1932, paints a picture of a cloned society devoted only to the pursuit of happiness.

David J. Triggle, Ph.D.
University Professor
School of Pharmacy and Pharmaceutical Sciences
State University of New York at Buffalo

1

The History of Opium and Morphine

On a cool, brisk, October morning, John wakes up, stumbles into the bathroom nauseous and dizzy, and begins his daily routine. As he looks at his unshaven, leathery face in the mirror, he realizes that today marks the five-year anniversary of the day he was wounded in battle, as well as the first day he was given morphine by medics to relieve the pain of the wound. Although, at first, this drug was very effective at lessening his discomfort, its pain-relieving properties dissipated with continued use. In fact, after years of morphine therapy, John was only left with an urge for the drug's euphoric effects. John, like many other wounded soldiers before him, has become an opiate addict. He begins each day like every other day. Specifically, he reaches into the bathroom cupboard, pulls out a wooden box, and begins to prepare his morphine injection.

THE OPIATES

Although this scenario represents an example of medical morphine use leading to addiction and dependence—an occurrence that is actually somewhat rare today—the potential for such effects are neither new nor surprising given this drug's origin. Interestingly, morphine is obtained from the same plant that produces opium, the poppy plant (Figure 1.1). Together, morphine and opium belong to a larger family of drugs named the **opiates**, which are known for producing a wide range of effects, from sedation to constipation.

Figure 1.1 Both opium and morphine are derived from a certain kind of poppy plant, shown here.

Today, however, they are most commonly used for the management of pain (Table 1.1).

Using opiates will result in a myriad of physiological and psychological effects. For example, in addition to pain relief,

Table 1.1 Selective List of Opiates

Morphine
Heroin
Hydromorphone
Oxymorphone
Codeine
Hydrocodone
Drocode
Oxycodone
Levorphanol
Methadone
Fentanyl
Nalbuphine
Propoxyphene
Buprenorphine
Pentazocine
Butorphanol

beneficial effects like anesthesia and relief from diarrhea occur when someone takes a single dose of morphine. The fact that opiates have the ability to produce effects like these clearly indicates that these drugs have a utility beyond the management of pain. Unfortunately, many of these effects will change with the continual use of these drugs. That is, chronic (long-term) opiate use reduces these drugs' ability to produce effects like pain relief and sedation. Moreover, continual opiate use can lead to addiction and dependence. In fact, for the addict, habitual opiate use can result in intense cravings for the drug, compulsive use, and, if abruptly stopped, withdrawal. To this end, the discovery and use of the opiates have been both a blessing that has benefited society and a plague that has affected many an unsuspecting user.

OPIATES AND THE BODY

The beneficial and detrimental effects of opiates result from their interaction with the ongoing biological processes within the body (see Chapters 3, 4, and 6). For example, opiates alter the functioning of specialized cells called **neurons**. Neurons are found in great abundance in the brain and spinal cord (the **central nervous system**), as well as in and around muscles, organs, and tissues (the **peripheral nervous system**. Neurons are specialized in that they can communicate with other neurons. The movement of information among neurons gives people the ability to sense and perceive things like temperature, light, and sound. Neuronal communication also allows us to experience emotions, think, and produce coordinated movement. Thus, by altering neuronal communication, opiates can affect our feelings, cognition, and behavior.

Opiates produce effects like pain relief and addiction by affecting subsets of neurons responsible for the sensation and perception of pain (see Chapter 6) and **euphoria** (a sense of well-being; see Chapter 5). Opiates produce their effects because they either enhance or lessen the neurons' ability to

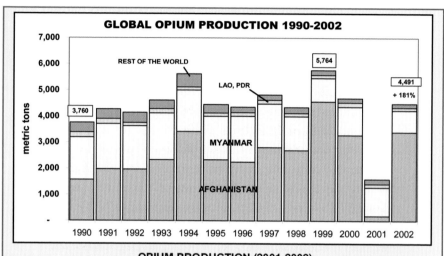

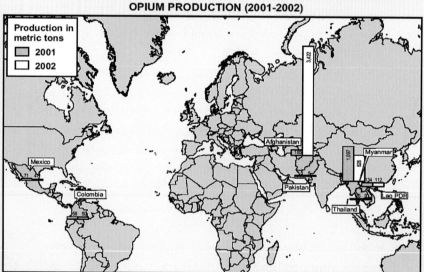

Figure 1.2 Top: global opium production in metric tons from 1990 to 2002. Afghanistan is the world's leading producer of opium, followed closely by Myanmar (formerly known as Burma). Other countries notorious for producing opium include Laos, Mexico, and Colombia. Bottom: global opium production in metric tons from 2001 to 2002 based on geographical location. Though opium was traditionally smuggled into North America from the Far East, opium production has been on the rise in Mexico and Colombia, decreasing the distance the drug has to travel to reach the United States.

convey information about these sensations to other neurons. The net result of this action is a deadening of pain and/or heightened sense of euphoria.

Opium and morphine have a long history of use both recreationally and medically, and, not surprisingly, opium production continues to rise (Figure 1.2). Reflection on the history and effects of these drugs has fueled a great desire to find alternatives to opium and morphine. In fact, this has been the guiding principle in opiate research: if alternatives to opium and morphine can be discovered and/or synthesized based on how opiates work within the body, it may be possible to use these new drugs to produce effects like pain relief without the accompanying risk of addiction and dependence. As you will see, the results have been mixed. Still, it is hard to imagine modern medicine without the opiates, given their integral place in the physician's toolbox.

> "Among all the remedies which it has pleased almighty God to give man to relieve his suffering, none is so universal and efficacious as opium."
>
> —Thomas Sydenham, considered to be the father of clinical medicine (circa 1680)

OPIUM

Morphine is one of the principal ingredients of opium, a drug that has been, by far, one of the most influential, popular, and commonly used and abused substances in human history. **Opium** is a naturally occurring drug that is cultivated directly from the **poppy** plant (*Papaver somniferum*; Figure 1.3). Poppy plants typically grow to a height of 3 or 4 feet. On top of the stalk, there is a large globe-like bulb that contains the seeds of the poppy plant. Surrounding the bulb are the petals of the poppy flower. Although the flowers vary based on species and growing conditions, the opium-producing poppy

Figure 1.3 The opium poppy is the source of opium, morphine, and heroin. Laborers incise the poppy pod, letting the opium sap seep out. The opium resin is then packaged into cakes and sent to the opium market.

plant is usually marked by the presence of white or purple flowers and a bulb that contains yellow seeds.

Although the poppy plant was at one time quite abundant throughout parts of Europe, the Middle East, and Asia, today only four countries—Australia, France, Spain, and Turkey—legitimately grow poppy plant crops for medicinal use. That is, these countries have been sanctioned to grow poppy plants by the United Nations International Narcotics Control Board in order to meet the world's opiate needs. This is not to say that poppy plant crops are not grown elsewhere. In fact, unregulated crops of poppy plants are found in great abundance in Myanmar (formerly known as Burma), Laos, Thailand, Afghanistan, Mexico, and Colombia. The production of opiates in these countries, however, is usually for illicit black-market trade rather than medicinal use.

The harvesting and selling of opium has not changed much over the past millennia. As the poppy plant ripens, the flowers that surround the poppy plant's pod fall off, exposing the bulb. Once this occurs, there is a noticeable drooping in the stalk of the plant. Laborers then quickly go into the poppy fields and methodically score the pods with a small harvesting blade. As a result of this process, the opium sap that resides within the pods (at this point, it is milky-white sap) will ooze out at the site of the incisions and adhere to the pod. During the next 12-hour period, the sap turns brown as it interacts with the air (that is, it oxidizes).

The next day, laborers then return to the fields and scrape the brown opium resin off the pods. After scraping, the opium resin is then packaged into cakes, which are shipped to and stored in large warehouses until it is time to send them to the opium market. At the market, the opium cakes are rated based on quality and purity, priced, and eventually bought by opium dealers. From the market, opium may be sent anywhere in the world where a demand for opium, morphine, or heroin (heroin is also made from opium) exists.

MEDICINAL AND RECREATIONAL OPIUM USE

For over a millennium, the ability of opium to immediately relieve pain, induce sleep, and stop diarrhea was matched by no other drug. For this reason, opium, and opium-laced tonics like **laudanum** (opium mixed with wine and spices) were very attractive medicines to both physicians and patients alike. In fact, most of the earlier references to the poppy plant and opium (from Sumerian, Egyptian, Greek, Roman, and Arab texts) indicate that people were keenly aware of the therapeutic benefits of this drug early in history. However, it is also clear that these earlier civilizations knew of opium's ability to produce euphoria, an effect that may lead to addiction and dependence.

The Sumerians (a society that thrived approximately 5,000 years ago) used the words *hul*, meaning "joy," and *gil*, meaning "plant," when referring to the poppy plant. This evidence suggests that it has been known for at least 5,000 years that ingesting opium would result in a euphoric sensation. There is also evidence that the ancient Greeks knew that the use of opium would quickly turn to misuse if it were not regulated in some way. For example, early Greek writings from Hippocrates and Galen indicate that, although poppy-based medicines were commonly used to ease pain and induce sleep, large enough quantities could produce dependence and death if this drug was not taken in a controlled manner. These writings clearly show that the Greeks knew that long-term opium use had the potential to result in intense cravings for the drug, compulsive use, and, if abruptly stopped, severe withdrawal symptoms.

Thus, although the practice of using opium as a medicine has been around for many years, the non-therapeutic qualities of this drug were realized early in its history. With no other drug available to match opium's potency and efficacy (its potential to produce maximal effects based on the dose of drug given), however, using opium as a medicine to treat ailments like pain, dysentery, and insomnia would remain popular for many centuries.

As the population of the world expanded and became more interconnected and industrialized over time, the medicinal use and subsequent abuse of opium (and laudanum) would increase as well, reaching a zenith in the 18th and 19th centuries (see "The Opium Wars" box). During this time period, there were several factors that contributed to the rapid spread of opium use and abuse throughout Asia, Europe, and North America. The frequent trading of goods between Europe and

THE OPIUM WARS

In the 18th century, the British loved Chinese tea, but had great difficulties obtaining this product. Given that the Chinese viewed all things foreign as barbaric, the value of British-borne products was somewhat limited to the Chinese. The answer to the British-Chinese trading problem would come in 1773, when British forces conquered the Bengal Province in India, then the world's leading producer of opium. With this victory, the British had a monopoly on the production and sale of opium. As such, the British now had an ideal commodity for trade with the Chinese.

Trading opium to China for Chinese goods proved quite a lucrative business for the British. The Chinese not only desired opium for its medicinal value, but soon for recreational purposes. Not surprisingly, as use of opium increased within the Chinese population, an opium epidemic would soon grip China. The Chinese Emperor responded to this problem by issuing an edict banning all opium use by the population. Unfortunately, this failed to curb the problem and, in 1839, the Emperor ordered Chinese forces to confiscate and burn all opium brought in by British ships. Thus, the Opium Wars began.

For approximately 3 years, the British and Chinese fought until, finally, British artillery and warships overwhelmed the Chinese forces. As a result of the loss, the Chinese were forced to capitulate both land and trading rights to the British. In fact, as a result of the Opium Wars, the island of Hong Kong would become a British colony until it was returned to Chinese control in 2000.

North America provided a means by which a lot of opium could cross the Atlantic Ocean in a relatively short period of time. Further, the United States' importation of cheap labor from the Asian labor market for the building of the railroads provided an impetus for the use and abuse of opium to spread westward across the country. Thus, the wonders and dangers of opium were introduced to many people by means of trade, societal expansion, and industrialization.

Given the alarming rate at which the incidence of opium use and abuse was increasing—opium was, in fact, popping up in medicine cabinets everywhere—it was not long before scientists of the 18th and 19th centuries began to search for alternatives to opium. Finding drugs that matched opium's ability to relieve pain and stop diarrhea, however, proved to be quite a difficult and elusive task, given that pharmacology (the science of how drugs work in the body) was still in its infancy and subject to much guesswork. Still, scientists believed that there was some basic "underlying principle" that gave opium its medicinal value. If this molecule could be isolated, it was believed that it would produce a far more potent and less addictive medicine than opium.

THE DISCOVERY OF MORPHINE

Although there is some dispute as to the exact date of the discovery, it is generally accepted by medical historians that the basis for opium's potent effects was discovered somewhere between the years 1805 and 1816 by Friedrich Wilhelm Sertürner. He was a pharmacist's assistant who was intent on learning why opium produced the effects that it did, that is, its underlying principle. As the story goes, Sertürner was able to isolate a yellowish-white crystalline compound from raw opium by immersing the drug in hot water and ammonia.

Unaware of what he had discovered, but curious about what its effects would be, Sertürner first tested his new discovery on some dogs (all of which died from the drug) and then, foolishly, on himself and three young boys. From this experiment, he chronicled that this new compound, like opium, could relieve pain and induce euphoria. However, it was also clear that, in sufficient doses, this compound would produce a **dysphoric** (that is, aversive) feeling, respiratory depression, nausea, vomiting, depression of the cough reflex, and constipation. In addition, he found that it was approximately ten times as potent as opium in relieving pain, so that less of the drug was needed to produce the same effect. Sertürner had indeed found opium's underlying principle. He would later name this new drug "morphine" after Morpheus, the Greek god of dreams.

MORPHINE AS A MEDICINE
As word of morphine's potency and potential as a medicine reached pharmaceutical companies, the commercial production of this drug quickly began in the mid-19th century. It was not only touted as an alternative to opium, but, surprisingly enough, as a cure for opium addiction and dependence. Its acceptance as a medicine, however, was staunchly resisted by a wary public for several reasons. A once naïve public had become all too keenly aware of the dangers of drug addiction and dependence. Specifically, both opium and cocaine addiction were widespread during this era. Further, at this time it was believed that addiction and dependence were phenomena that resulted from ingesting (and digesting) drugs rather than by the direct effects of the drugs in the brain. In fact, most medicines of that time were administered as tonics (like laudanum) or as snuffs (like cocaine) and produced high degrees of addiction and dependence. Thus, morphine was not going to be accepted as a medicine until a suitable and alternative delivery method for the drug could be found.

The situation with morphine changed in 1853 when a new invention called the hypodermic needle was perfected.

Back in the 1800s, hypodermic needles were made of a combination of glass and metal (unlike the modern, disposable plastic syringes of today). Specifically, the original hypodermic needles comprised a large glass tube, which held the drug solution, with a wide opening at one end and a narrow opening at the other end. At the narrow opening of the tube, a needle would be attached that was sharp enough to puncture the skin with minimal damage. At the large opening of the tube, either a metal or glass plunger would be inserted to push the drug solution through the needle. Thus, drugs would no longer have to be taken orally but could rather be injected directly into the body at a specific location. Surprisingly, such an invention lessened the public's skepticism about taking newly developed drugs like morphine.

With the advent of the hypodermic needle, morphine as a medicine was quite effective; for example, it was used to relieve pain and diarrhea experienced by soldiers living in deplorable conditions while at war. It was neither long nor surprising, however, before the addictive potential of morphine began to appear. Soldiers who were given morphine during times of war would come back to society addicted and dependent on the drug. In fact, morphine dependence would soon earn the nickname "Soldier's Disease." Furthermore, morphine addiction and dependence would quickly spread throughout the general public. In fact, as acceptance of morphine and its new delivery method grew, vials of morphine and hypodermic needle kits would begin popping up in medicine cabinets throughout society. Morphine addiction and dependence knew no social class or boundaries. As such, another drug pandemic gripped society—but this time, morphine.

In response to the growing morphine problem, as well as the prohibitionist movement of the early 20th century (prohibitionists preached about the morality of drug use and believed in a doctrine of complete sobriety), governments around the world quickly passed tough legislation (such as the

Harrison Narcotics Act passed by Congress in 1914) restricting the recreational use of morphine. That is, although morphine could be used by the public, it could no longer be freely distributed without proper documentation and taxation. Approximately 60 years later, Congress passed even tougher legislation with the Controlled Substance Act of 1970, wherein morphine, among other drugs, would become a scheduled (or mostly prohibited) compound. Individuals caught possessing morphine without a prescription faced large fines and, perhaps, jail time. According to the Controlled Substance Act, morphine is a "Schedule II" drug:

> The drug has a high potential for abuse, an accepted medical use in treatment in the United States or a currently accepted medical use with severe restrictions. Abuse may lead to severe psychological or physical dependence.

> Other examples of Schedule II drugs include Dilaudid®, Demerol®, methadone, cocaine, and PCP. Today, morphine remains a Schedule II compound, only to be used by patients under the supervision of physicians and in a narrow set of circumstances.

MORPHINE TODAY

The medicinal use of morphine remains an integral, but strictly regulated, part of clinical medicine. In fact, morphine is commonly used in hospitals for the management of post-operative and chronic pain. Morphine has also been the basis for a variety of new drugs similar in chemical makeup. For example, the U.S. Drug Enforcement Administration (DEA) estimates that out of the 130 to 140 tons of morphine imported into the United States annually, only 15% is used as is. The remaining 85% of morphine stock is converted to other popular morphine-based medicines, such as hydromorphone (Dilaudid®), oxymorphone (Numorphan®), methadone

(Dolophine®), and oxycodone (Roxicodone®, Percodan®, Percocet®). Together, these drugs are classified as either the opiates (opiates are drugs that work in the same manner and produce similar effects as opium) or narcotics (derived from the Greek word for "make numb").

2

The Movement of Morphine Through the Body

Morphine is capable of producing a variety of both beneficial and detrimental effects in humans. For example, morphine is an excellent pain reliever (**analgesic**), a distinct benefit, but it also has a high rate of addiction and dependence. These effects are due to morphine's interaction with a number of biological systems within the human body. A basic understanding of how drugs are administered and move through the body is necessary to understand how morphine works.

MORPHINE ADMINISTRATION

For morphine to produce an effect (such as pain relief), the drug must be delivered to the specific cellular system within the body that mediates that effect. More specifically, morphine must interact with the neurons in the brain and/or spinal cord that mediate the sensation and perception of pain in order to alter one's response to a painful stimulus (see Chapter 4).

The method of introducing a drug into the body is generically referred to as the drug's **route of administration**. There are several ways in which morphine, as well as other opiates, can be administered. For example, they can be given by mouth in the form of a pill or liquid, which is called the oral route of administration. The oral route is commonly used because it is a convenient and relatively safe way for people to take a drug. Drugs can also be administered through the rectum as a suppository, though understandably people are often much more hesitant to take a drug this way. As noted, drugs are also given by an injection with a hypodermic needle into the muscle (intramuscularly), under the outer layer of skin (subcutaneously), or into a vein (intravenously; Table 2.1). Although people usually don't administer drugs to themselves by these means, these routes do provide a level of control in the delivery of drugs not afforded to by many of the other methods (see "Patient-Controlled Administration of Morphine" box). Specifically, injecting drugs ensures that their absorption and distribution throughout the body is more complete than would occur with swallowing a pill.

Other routes of drug administration include through the skin by a patch (transdermally), through the nasal cavity as a spray (intranasally), or by placing a pill under the tongue (sublingually). Finally, many drugs such as general anesthetics are given by inhalation in a gaseous form. Although many opiates like codeine and oxycodone are commonly administered orally in the form of a pill, morphine itself is most often administered by intravenous injection.

MORPHINE DISTRIBUTION IN THE BODY

If morphine is successfully delivered into the body via one of the routes of administration, it must leave the site of administration and distribute throughout the body in order to produce the desired effect. Most of the pain-relieving and euphoric effects of opiates like morphine are mediated by central nervous system mechanisms (by cells in the brain and/or spinal cord) rather than by peripheral mechanisms (the site of tissue damage causing the pain). Since morphine and other opiates are typically administered peripherally as a pill or by injection rather than directly into the brain, sufficient levels of the drug

Table 2.1 Pros and Cons of Different Routes of Administration

ROUTE	BENEFITS	DISADVANTAGES
Oral	It is convenient, painless, and easy to do.	Can be broken down rapidly and interact with food. Further, a pill cannot be swallowed if the patient is unconscious.
Sublingual	There is rapid distribution throughout the body. There is little breakdown of the drug.	Its effects are lost if the drug is swallowed. Only a small dose can be administered.
Rectal	There is little breakdown of the drug by the liver. Has utility with children.	Drug absorption is erratic and this method is uncomfortable.
Inhalation	There is little breakdown of the drug by the liver. Absorption is rapid and controllable.	High risk of overdose.
Injection, Intramuscular	Can administer a large volume of the drug. The effects can be sustained for a long period of time.	Must be trained to administer. The sites of injection are limited.
Injection, Subcutaneous	Can be administered by the patient. There is slow but complete absorption.	It is painful and tissue damage may occur.
Injection, Intravenous	There is rapid effect.	There is high risk of overdose.

must distribute from the site of administration to the target area responsible for the biological function.

The most efficient way to distribute a drug throughout the body is to exploit the fact that blood must be delivered to and from every area in the body for the body to survive. This feat is accomplished via the circulatory system and its principle organ, the heart (Figure 2.1). Thus, a drug can distribute

PATIENT-CONTROLLED ADMINISTRATION OF MORPHINE

Although morphine continues to be commonly administered to patients by intravenous injection, new technology has enabled the patient to have control over their own pain management. Today, patient-controlled analgesia (PCA) allows pain sufferers to administer morphine intravenously to themselves with the push of a button. Patients who are in pain can be connected to a PCA pump that will deliver morphine intravenously on demand.

The amount of morphine delivered is based on a self-reported level of pain (usually on a scale of 1 to 10). After the patient rates the pain that they are experiencing, a physician will determine what dose and how frequently the morphine can be self-administered. This is accomplished by programming the pump to only administer the drug following a pre-determined time interval. In other words, the patient will not overdose on the drug, given that the button will only deliver morphine after a certain amount of time has elapsed.

One downfall to this method is that a PCA pump is very expensive, limiting its use to hospital settings. Further, patients may still experience discomfort because they are sleeping and can't push the button. Still, PCA has become one of the leading methods of pain management in hospital settings.

throughout the body by hitching a ride with the natural flow of blood within the body.

Although this concept seems simple and is the basis for the distribution of most drugs, including opiates, there are several roadblocks that can make this journey quite difficult. For example, if a drug is taken orally, as in the case of codeine, it must first survive the acidic environment of the stomach.

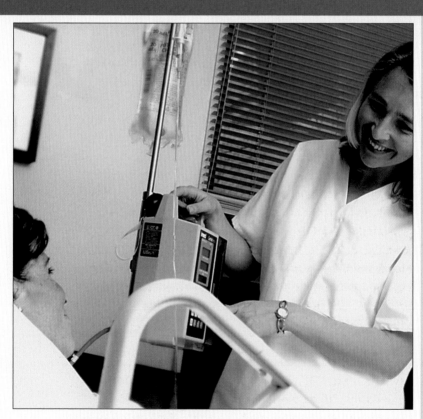

This nurse is setting up an intravenous (IV) line for her patient. Patient-controlled analgesia (PCA) allows pain sufferers to administer morphine to themselves intravenously.

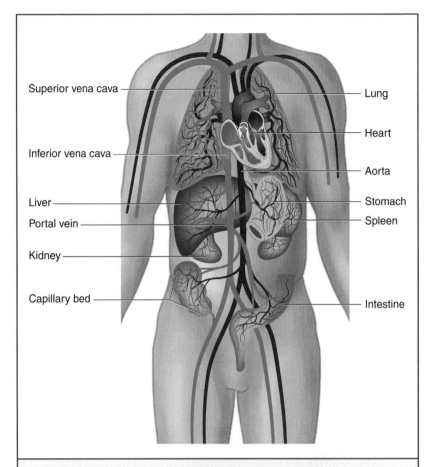

Figure 2.1 The human blood circulatory system. Blood is pumped from the heart to every area of the body, making it an ideal drug distribution system. In fact, the heart is actually capable of pumping the entire blood volume throughout the body in approximately 60 seconds, allowing drugs to be quickly delivered to the remotest body regions.

Gastric acids are quite efficient at destroying most substances, including drugs, so there may be some loss of drug in the stomach. If some of the administered drug is lost in the stomach by gastric acid breakdown, then the amount of drug circulating throughout the body is lessened. This may limit the amount of drug that will eventually reach the intended cellular target.

Even if most of the drug survives the gastric environment, in order to reach the bloodstream the drug molecule must be able to cross the stomach's tissue lining as well as the walls of blood vessels and other types of cells. Given the chemical makeup of drugs and the composition of the membranes that surround many of these biological structures, many drugs have only a limited capacity to cross these barriers. So, these factors may reduce the amount of circulating drug by trapping a portion of total drug either in the stomach or in the intracellular space (the space between cells).

If all these initial barriers are crossed, there may be other roadblocks encountered on the drug's journey to the target cells. For example, once a drug is circulating in the bloodstream, it may be at risk of being destroyed or incapacitated by enzymes or other proteins that naturally occur in the bloodstream. Some of these proteins can attach to the drug molecule, tagging it as a foreign substance so that it can be broken down and eliminated from the body.

Finally, the drug molecule must be able to again pass through the walls of the blood vessels and other cellular barriers to reach the final, intended biological target. Thus, in order to produce the desired effects, an opiate may naturally have to be able to bypass or avoid these barriers, be designed with these barriers in mind, or administered in doses sufficient to ensure that a clinically significant amount of drug will pass through these barriers and reach the intended target.

In the context of morphine distribution, many of these barriers can be quickly bypassed by administering the drug directly into the bloodstream. This ensures that a sufficient level of morphine will reach, for instance, the pain centers in the brain. Thus, the effects of stomach acids, tissue barriers, and enzymatic breakdown become less of a factor in morphine's distribution.

MORPHINE METABOLISM

Other factors beside the route of administration and drug distribution can influence morphine's ability to reach its biological target. Among these is the rate at which the body **metabolizes** (breaks down) the drug. As mentioned above, drug metabolism can occur through the interaction of drug molecules with enzymes. These enzymes actually act to alter the chemical structure of the drug molecule. Specifically, the process of metabolism involves turning an active drug (that is, one that produces a biological effect like pain relief) into an inactive drug, or vice versa. The metabolism of morphine begins the moment the drug is taken. This process occurs within the bloodstream as well as in the kidneys and liver. In fact, the kidneys and liver act as the body's natural blood filtration system, primarily charged with the removal of foreign substances, like drugs, from the bloodstream.

Drug metabolism plays a significant role in altering morphine's ability to produce effects (Figure 2.2). For example, morphine goes through extensive metabolism in the liver when initially distributing throughout the body. This phenomenon is called "first-pass metabolism" and has been suggested to reduce the levels of circulating morphine by approximately 75%. If this is not taken into account when calculating the dose, the result will be a lessening of the likelihood that morphine will distribute to its site of action and produce the desired effect.

Alternatively, morphine metabolism may also increase its ability to produce effects like pain relief. Specifically, morphine can be broken down into both active and inactive **metabolites** (a metabolite is a byproduct of drug breakdown). One of the active metabolites of morphine is called **morphine-6-glucuronide**. Through experimentation, scientists have demonstrated that this metabolite is twice as potent as morphine at relieving pain when administered systemically (into the bloodstream) and 1,000 times as potent as morphine when administered directly into the brain. For this reason, many scientists believe

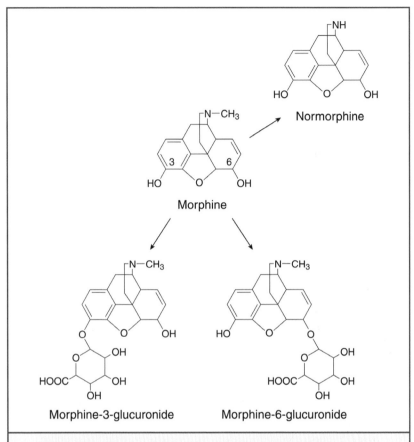

Figure 2.2 The metabolic pathway for morphine. Morphine can be broken down into both active and inactive metabolites. The inactive metabolite of morphine is normorphine. The active morphine metabolites include morphine-3-glucuronide and morphine-6-glucuronide. Morphine-6-glucurinide is 1,000 times as potent as morphine in relieving pain when injected directly into the brain.

that the levels of pain relief that patients report after the administration of morphine is actually due to the metabolite morphine-6-glucuronide rather than morphine itself.

Taking morphine repeatedly may actually change the rate of morphine metabolism. For example, the body may become more efficient at breaking down morphine over time. In other words, metabolic drug tolerance may occur with repeated drug administration. Therefore, a greater dose of morphine may be needed to produce the same effect that a lower dose achieved at a previous point in time. Conversely, the body may also become less efficient at metabolizing morphine, resulting in a phenomenon called **metabolic sensitization**. Here, drug levels rise in the blood as the body loses its ability to break down the compound. Therefore, sensitization results in a stronger drug effect than occurred with the same dose of drug previously.

MORPHINE ELIMINATION

In addition to the administration, distribution, and metabolism of morphine, the rate at which the body eliminates the drug also influences morphine's ability to produce an effect. Like drug metabolism, morphine elimination begins the instant the drug is administered, meaning a portion of a morphine dose given to an individual is actually eliminated from the body before it has the ability to produce its effect. Although most drugs are eliminated by the kidneys, leaving the body though the urine, drugs can also be eliminated through sweating and when a person exhales.

In comparison to many drugs, morphine is eliminated from the body rather quickly. Specifically, 90% of morphine leaves the body within the first 24 hours after administration (drugs like antidepressants or marijuana can remain in the body for weeks). Most morphine is eliminated via urine rather than by other routes.

Together, it is clear that the route of drug administration, its distribution, metabolism, and excretion play a significant role in determining how effective morphine, as well as other opiates, are in producing their effects. Despite these factors, however, morphine and the other opiates remain the most effective and commonly used medicines in combating pain.

3

Morphine's Effect on the Nervous System

It is the interaction of morphine with the ongoing biological processes of the body that is responsible for its ability to produce effects like pain relief and/or addiction. Specifically, morphine produces its effect by altering the functioning of neurons. Neurons are specialized cells found within the body. Together, these cells form the human nervous system. It should be noted that there are two main divisions of this system: neurons within the brain and spinal cord make up the central nervous system, whereas neurons that reside outside these structures make up the peripheral nervous system.

Neurons are unique from other human cells (like skin cells) for several reasons. First, they possess the ability to detect information about the outside world and then send it to other neurons. For example, sensory neurons are charged primarily with "sensing" the sights and sounds of the environment and are found predominately in the peripheral nervous system. Sensory neurons send information about the outside world to other neurons within the spinal cord, which, in turn, send signals to neurons in the brain. That is, sensory neurons communicate with neurons that reside within the central nervous system.

Once this information has reached the brain, it will be deciphered, and a **precept** of the world will be formed (a precept is a mental representation of the external environment). Neurons are able to accomplish this feat because there are billions of neurons and trillions of connections between them. We are capable of perceiving our world because groups of neurons tend to form separate yet integrated systems within the brain (Table 3.1). For example, in addition to neurons responsible for sight and sound, other groups of neurons in the brain are responsible for smell, touch, and pain. And other brain neurons are responsible for things like emotion, memory, and/or euphoria. Interestingly, these brain areas all communicate with one another, so that sights, sounds, feelings, and memories are all integrated to form a single precept of the world.

It is important to note that neurons within the brain also communicate with other neurons within the peripheral nervous system. These neurons are motor neurons responsible for producing movement. Information sent from the brain, through the spinal cord, and eventually to motor neurons gives us the ability to walk, run, talk, and eat. Thus, our interpretation and negotiation through the world is made possible through discrete neuronal connections working in concert.

As a concrete example of how the human nervous system works, if you accidentally place your hand on a hot stove, neurons that respond to heat (thermal-responsive sensory neurons) become excited. Because these neurons are now active, they send signals to other neurons in your brain that, first, interpret the event as painful and significant, and, second, produce a reflexive movement to pull your hand away from the hot stove. Because of this activity, your body will be saved from an extensive thermal injury.

Together, neuronal communication mediates our sensation and perception of stimuli, as well as our behavior in response to those stimuli. The fact that neurons act and communicate in this fashion make them an ideal target for psychoactive drugs such as morphine—drugs that affect our sensation, perception, and behavior.

COMMUNICATION BETWEEN NEURONS

Morphine produces its effect by altering the communication

Table 3.1 Brain Regions and Functions

REGION	FUNCTION
Frontal cortex	Involved in planning, thinking, and decision-making
Motor cortex	Controls movements of the face, arms, and legs
Sensory cortex	Involved in the perception of touch
Visual cortex	Processes sight and vision
Cerebellum	Controls motor coordination, balance
Brain stem	Controls basic bodily functions, such as chewing, swallowing, heart rate, and breathing
Hypothalamus	Controls metabolism, sleep, eating, and drinking
Limbic system*	Controls memory, emotions, and motivation

* The limbic system is made up of several brain structures, such as the hippocampus, amygdala, and basal forebrain.

between neurons. A neuron's ability to communicate is partly a product of its structure and partly a product of its function. Neurons, like all cells, have a cell body that contains a nucleus as well as other machinery responsible for sustaining the life of the cell (the mitochondria, ribosomes, etc.). Unlike other cells, however, neurons have tubular branch-like protrusions that emanate from the cell body called dendrites and axons. The **dendrites** are mostly responsible for receiving signals from other neurons. The ability of dendrites to detect these incoming signals results from the fact that they have specialized proteins called receptors positioned all along their length. As such, dendrites are much like radio antennas with microwave dishes on them—they rise into the intracellular space from the cell body in order to receive signals from other neurons.

Like dendrites, **axons** are also branch-like protrusions that originate from the cell body. These structures, however, are chiefly responsible for sending signals to other neurons. Specifically, axons are capable of sending signals over vast distances because they wind their way through the central and peripheral nervous systems, terminating in close proximity to dendrites of other neurons. In other words, axons are like telephone wires, carrying a signal from one phone to the next. Of special note, the axons and dendrites of neurons usually do not come in direct contact with one another. Rather, a microscopic gap called a **synapse** exists between these structures.

In terms of function, neurons transmit information about sensations, perceptions, and behaviors through electrical and chemical events. These electrical and chemical events begin in the dendrites of a neuron, move through the cell body, and eventually down and out of the axon. When a neuron's dendritic receptor receives a signal from another neuron or detects stimuli from the external environment, electrical charges (which consist of charged molecules like sodium or potassium) enter the cell body. This internal electrical charge, now called

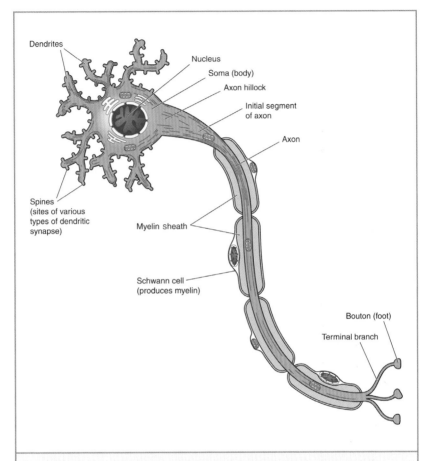

Dendrites

Nucleus

Soma (body)

Axon hillock

Initial segment
of axon

Axon

Spines
(sites of various
types of dendritic
synapse)

Myelin sheath

Schwann cell
(produces myelin)

Bouton (foot)

Terminal branch

Figure 3.1 The main structural components of a neuron are its dendrites, cell body, and axon. Signals are received from other neurons at the dendrites and this information is sent down the axon. Neurons are not in direct contact with one another; rather, they are separated by a microscopic gap called a synapse.

an action potential, is then sent streaming down the axon away from the cell body (Figures 3.1 and 3.2). When this action potential reaches the end of the axon (the terminal), it triggers the release of a chemical—a **neurotransmitter**—into the synaptic space. Given the close proximity of one neuron's axon and another neuron's dendrites, the neurotransmitter molecules

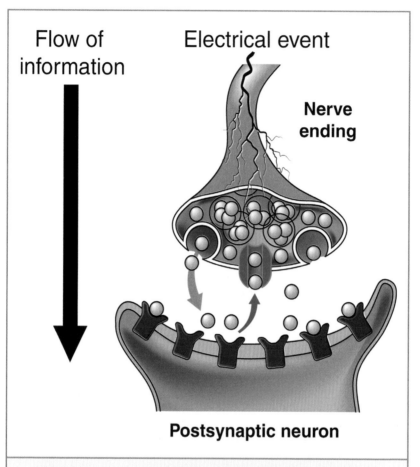

Flow of information

Electrical event

Nerve ending

Postsynaptic neuron

Figure 3.2 Neurons communicate with one another by electrical and chemical processes. When a neuron receives a signal from another neuron, it reprocesses this information into an internal electrical charge called an action potential. This electrical charge travels down the axon until it reaches the terminal. Here, the electrical charge causes the release of special chemicals called neurotransmitters into the synapse.

are able to travel across the synapse and attach to the neighboring neuron's dendritic receptors (see Figure 3.2). Then, the electrical and chemical process starts all over again, allowing the signal to continue.

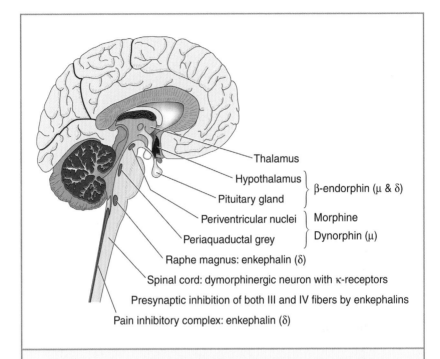

Thalamus

Hypothalamus ⎫
⎬ β-endorphin (μ & δ)
Pituitary gland ⎭

Periventricular nuclei ⎫
⎬ Morphine
Periaquaductal grey ⎭ Dynorphin (μ)

Raphe magnus: enkephalin (δ)

Spinal cord: dymorphinergic neuron with κ-receptors

Presynaptic inhibition of both III and IV fibers by enkephalins

Pain inhibitory complex: enkephalin (δ)

Figure 3.3 The distribution of opioid receptors throughout the human central nervous system by receptor type. There are three general types of opioid receptors: the mu (designated by the Greek letter μ) receptor found throughout the brain and spinal cord; the kappa (κ) receptor found predominately in the brain (specifically, the hypothalamus); and the delta (δ) receptor located in certain sections of the spinal cord. Morphine's pain-relieving and euphoric activities appear to be mediated mostly by the mu receptor.

MORPHINE AND THE OPIOID SYSTEM

How does morphine affect neuronal communication? First, it is important to understand that if specific groups of neurons communicate with one another to produce sensations, perceptions, and behaviors, and morphine has the ability to alter the neuronal communication within these systems, then sensations, perceptions, and behaviors may be affected by the interaction of morphine and neurons. In fact, this is how morphine works.

Morphine affects neurons that have certain types of receptors on them, called opioid receptors. Neurons with such a receptor are broadly classified into the **opioid system** (*opiate* is the term used to classify drugs that work on the opioid system). The opioid system does not work in isolation of other neurons but rather in concert with other neuronal systems. Once opioid receptors are activated, these neurons release neurotransmitters that shut down the ability of other neurons to talk with one another, inhibiting neuronal communication. The net result of this activity can be the alteration in the sensation and perception of pain (see Chapter 4), as well as the development and maintenance of addictive behaviors (see Chapter 6).

Morphine's ability to affect this system is due to the fact that morphine, on a molecular level, can act in the same manner as some of the natural neurotransmitters (chemical messengers) involved in opioid neuronal communication. That is, morphine acts as an opioid agonist at the dendritic receptor. An **opioid agonist** is a drug that mimics the effects of the opioid peptides. The opioid peptides include the neurotransmitters **enkephalin**, **endorphin**, and **dynorphin**. These neurotransmitters are considered the "key" for the opioid receptor's "lock"—they are specific for the opioid receptor, and vice versa. Given that morphine is an opioid agonist, and opioid peptides naturally shut down neuronal activity once attached to an opioid receptor, morphine will also shut down (or produce an inhibitory effect on) neuronal communication. Therefore, morphine is an agonist with inhibitory action at the level of the neuron, reducing the potential of one neuron to talk to the next neuron.

There are three general types of opioid receptors. There is the mu receptor (designated by the Greek letter μ, which is found throughout the brain and spinal cord. There is the kappa receptor (designated by the Greek letter κ), which is found predominately in the brain. There is also the delta receptor (designated by the Greek letter δ), which is located in certain sections of the spinal cord (see Figure 3.3). Morphine produces pronounced effects via its activity at the mu, kappa, and delta receptors. Specifically, morphine's pain-relieving and euphoric activity appear to be mediated by the mu receptor, more so than by the others. Activity at the kappa receptor by morphine, on the other hand, has been linked to the aversive feeling that can result with morphine use. Furthermore, delta-receptor activation by morphine is responsible for side effects like respiratory depression.

Although the ability of morphine to attach to some of these receptors is a critical component involved in its ability to produce effects such as pain relief, the nonspecificity of morphine for other opioid receptors results in the alteration of a host of bodily functions, including dysphoric feelings, changes in respiration, blood pressure, body temperature, and feeding.

4

Morphine and Pain

"The art of life is the art of avoiding pain."

—Thomas Jefferson

We have all experienced pain at some point in time. In fact, pain is an inevitable and necessary part of life. Pain tells us that we are hurt. Without pain, we would have difficulty avoiding situations that were dangerous to us. Thus, pain is essential to our survival.

Although "pain" as a concept may seem simple—a result of an event that causes significant distress to an individual—it is actually a very complex phenomenon with a myriad of physiological, behavioral, and subjective (interpretational) components. The term *pain* is used by individuals to describe a variety of events and circumstances. For instance, some people describe an emotional event (like ending a relationship with a boyfriend or girlfriend) as a "painful" experience. Others use the term to describe a person that is annoying to them (you're "being a pain"). Further, "pain" can also be used to describe sensory and perceptual phenomena that result from a physical injury. Although it would be ideal if a single drug, like morphine, could reduce all the pain that people experience in the world—emotional, physical, or both—the ability of morphine to function as a pain reliever appears to be specific to the unpleasant sensory and perceptual event resulting from physical trauma to the body.

THE SENSATION AND PERCEPTION
OF PHYSICAL PAIN

As noted, physical pain most often results from some sort of injury to the body. This injury may be thermal, chemical, and/or mechanical in nature. For example, burning one's hand on a stove is a thermal injury, whereas getting sprayed with pepper spray is a chemical insult. Hitting one's shin on a coffee table would be considered a mechanical injury. Regardless, all result in either irritation and/or tissue damage and eventually lead to the perception of pain.

The body has highly adapted neuronal systems to deal with the sensation and perception of pain (also known as **nociceptive nerve pathways**). Structurally, this system can be conceptualized as beginning in the peripheral areas of the body, for example, the skin around the feet (Figure 4.1). It then travels through the spinal cord and eventually terminates in the brain. Pain detectors, which are nothing more than free nerve endings (specialized dendrites), lie within the layers of the skin. These receptors are highly responsive to thermal, chemical, and/or mechanical stimuli. For example, these nerves will become active when exposed to hot and cold temperatures, in the presence of chemicals absorbing through the skin, as well as with the occurrence of pressure and physical damage brought on by cuts and scrapes (Figure 4.2).

It should also be noted that these nerve endings can also become active via the physiological changes that occur within the body following an injury. So, although bruising and swelling are indicators that the body is beginning to repair itself, the fluid that causes bruising and swelling contains chemicals, such as prostaglandins, that sensitize the pain detectors. (Have you ever bruised your shin and then bumped it on the edge of a coffee table? It really hurts.) Thus, the pain we perceive following an injury not only results from the initial insult (called immediate pain), but also from the healing

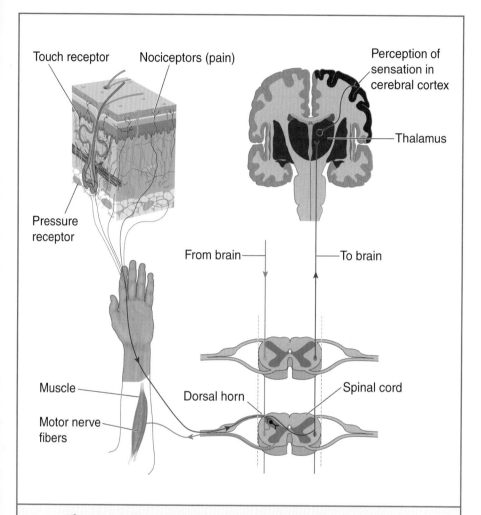

Figure 4.1 The nociceptive nerve pathway is one of the major ascending pain pathways in the human body. Pain detectors in the periphery detect painful stimuli and send signals to the pain "fibers." Pain fibers leave the periphery and enter the spinal cord at the dorsal horn, synapsing onto the ascending neuronal spinal tract. These neurons then carry the information to the thalamus. From the thalamus, neurons send information to the higher centers of the brain, such as the association and somatosensory cortices, allowing us to perceive where and what kind of pain we are experiencing.

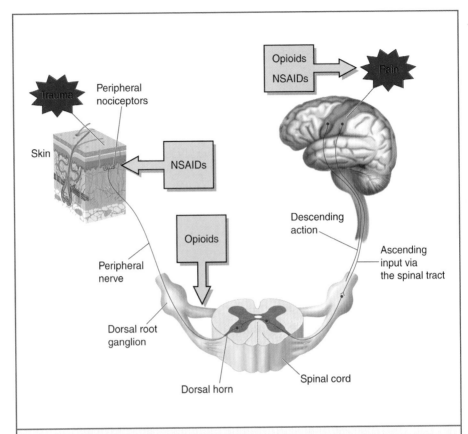

Figure 4.2 Pain fibers travel through this pain pathway via neurons that carry the information to the limbic system, allowing us to perceive that a "bad" event has just occurred.

process that begins immediately after the injury has occurred (called secondary or chronic pain).

Regardless of how pain detectors are stimulated (either by thermal, chemical, or mechanical stimuli, and/or bruising), they all communicate with a common mechanism that eventually sends pain signals to the brain. Following an injury, the pain detectors send signals about pain to a class of neurons referred to as the pain "fibers." There are multiple types of pain fibers that serve to decipher the type, quality, and/or intensity of the pain stimuli experienced. For instance, the relative activity of pain fibers will encode for thermal, chemical, or mechanical stimuli, stinging or stabbing pain, as well as low- versus high-intensity insults. This is quite a feat given all the different combinations of "pain" people can feel, but it involves releasing the neurotransmitters **glutamate** and **substance P** at different rates and quantities based on the stimuli experienced.

To illustrate this point, imagine a low-intensity stimulus like an itch. Our ability to distinguish an itch from a broken bone results from the fact that pain fibers release only a minute amount of glutamate and substance P at a low frequency with the itch. Alternatively, pain fibers may release a massive amount of glutamate and substance P at a high frequency following a broken arm. Thus, these fibers are highly adept at deciphering and transmitting information to the central nervous system (the brain and spinal cord) about the type and quality of pain that is being experienced.

Once in the spinal cord, pain fibers will synapse (in other words, communicate) with the neurons that form the ascending spinal tracts (see Figures 4.1 and 4.2). They are "ascending" because their axons begin at the lower areas of the spinal cord and travel up to the brain. Some of the ascending neuronal spinal tracts terminate in the **thalamus**, an area of the brain that is considered the gatekeeper for most information entering the higher areas of the cortex. Alternatively, some of the ascending neuronal spinal tracts also travel up the spinal cord and terminate in the limbic system, an area of the brain responsible for emotion.

From the thalamus, pain information is sent to areas of the brain that perceive the type and location of pain experienced. These brain areas are referred to as the **somatosensory** and **association cortices**. Limbic activation by pain stimuli adds an emotional component to the perception of pain: it will tell us that a "bad" event has just occurred. Thus, the sensation and perception of pain occurs in related, but anatomically distinct, places in the human nervous system (see "Phantom Pain" box). This concept is important when discussing how morphine reduces pain.

OPIOID PEPTIDES, MORPHINE, AND PAIN RELIEF

The body is capable of altering the perception of pain on its own, though its effectiveness is somewhat limited. This phenomenon is due primarily to the release of the opioid peptides, their activity on opioid receptors, and the subsequent inhibition of neuronal communication

PHANTOM PAIN

People who have had limbs amputated sometimes report that they perceive the limb to be still attached, despite their knowing that it has been removed. Moreover, they may actually feel the sensation of pain in the missing limb. Such phenomena are called phantom limb syndrome and phantom pain syndrome, respectively.

Phantom sensations can actually be quite debilitating to the amputee if severe enough. Although it is unknown what causes this perception, many possibilities exist. For example, some scientists have suggested that frayed and scarred nerve endings send out abnormal signals to the brain, which are then interpreted as coming from the missing appendage. Others believe that the brain areas responsible for interpreting information from a missing limb (like a hand) come under the control of neurons that are responsible for sensing other parts of the body, like the face. Thus, any activity brought on by sensations in the face (wind blowing across your face) would also activate the areas responsible for the missing hand. Regardless, the phantom syndromes give us unique insight into the inner workings of the human nervous system and the mind.

following opioid neuron activation. Therefore, it should not be surprising that pain neurons, as described earlier, overlap and communicate with neurons that have opioid receptors on them, in both the peripheral and central nervous systems.

For instance, when an individual is in pain, he or she will experience a state of stress. Stress actually causes the release of opioid peptides from neurons and glands (such as the pituitary gland). These peptides will, in turn, quickly circulate throughout the body and eventually attach to the mu receptors on opioid neurons. Once these peptides are attached, the opioid neurons become active with electrical and chemical activity. Because

A SURVIVOR'S STORY

"While morphine protects the brain from perceiving physical trauma, it also alters the perception of reality. I was given the unfortunate opportunity to struggle through a morphine-induced coma. During a near-fatal house fire, I sustained third-degree burns over 30% of my body. The immediate physical pain in such a situation is far too much for the brain to comprehend, so morphine must be administered to block its effects. After my initial dose of morphine, I was kept 'under' on morphine for approximately 10 weeks. Throughout those 10 weeks, my friends and family were always at my side. Much of the time, I showed no outward signs of discomfort and my visitors considered me to be coherent—even joyful—but I only remember being afraid. I can recall several recurring environments and scenarios, all of which were based on repressed phobias and traumatic memories. Any information I received from my physical environment was instantly added to a hellish nightmare I was constantly trying to pull myself out of."

—Jeffrey Thompson, Portland, Oregon

opioid neurons are inhibitory, they send signals in the form of neurotransmitters to both pain fibers and the ascending spinal pain tracts. These signals block the transmission of the pain signal from reaching the brain. Thus, although the actual sensation of the painful event still occurs, the signal indicating that one is in pain will never reach the areas of the brain charged with interpreting that signal.

Morphine works much like these opioid peptides do. Specifically, morphine is an opioid agonist, mimicking the effects of the opioid peptides at the level of the neuron. So, morphine itself can attach to the mu receptors and block the neuronal pain signal from reaching the brain. This is quite eloquently illustrated when people describe the effects of morphine while in pain (see "A Survivor's Story" box). When on morphine, people report that the sensation of pain is still there, but they no longer seem to care about the pain they are experiencing.

GENDER, PAIN, AND PAIN RELIEF

There are many behavioral and biological differences between men and women. Interestingly, these sex differences also extend to how men and women respond to pain and pain medications like morphine. For instance, it has been reported that women often describe a standardized pain stimulus as more intense, longer in duration, and more debilitating than that which is described by men. Further, women have also been reported to have a lower threshold for pain then males. That is, women can experience pain when presented with a stimulus that males are unable to detect. Although there are sex differences in relation to male versus female responsiveness to pain, these differences only emerge in adolescence and wane by early adulthood.

In the context of the male versus female response to pain medications like morphine, sex differences are less clear.

For example, the prevalence of prescription pain medication use is often reported as greater for females than in males. Further, females often need more morphine than males to achieve the same degree of analgesia. Alternatively, males often consume more PCA-administered morphine than females in the first day following a major surgical procedure.

Although it is unknown why there are such sex differences in pain and pain management, several possibilities exist. First, females often cognitively cope with pain in a different manner than males. For example, women may be vocal about the pain they are experiencing and seek more social support to deal with their pain. This process may actually make the pain experience more salient and conscious for females than in males. Secondly, there is much greater hormonal variability in females (due to the menstrual cycle) than in males. These variations may, in part, determine how responsive females are to pain and pain medications like morphine. In addition to these hormonal differences, the onset and duration of morphine-induced analgesia differs between males and females. Specifically, females report a slower onset and offset of morphine-induced analgesia as compared to their male counterparts. These differences may alter the morphine's effectiveness at relieving pain. Gender is a factor that will determine one's response to pain and pain medications like morphine.

SUMMARY

Although there are many forms of physical pain that people can experience, a highly specialized neuronal system has evolved within the human body to detect, decipher, and respond to pain. Morphine is a highly effective analgesic because of its ability to enhance the body's natural defense against pain. Morphine's pain-relieving abilities stem from its similarity to opioid peptides and, thus, its activity on the opioid system. The net result of this action is to stop the pain signal from reaching the areas of the brain charged with interpreting that signal.

5

Alternatives to Morphine in Managing Pain

Today, morphine is not the only drug available to manage pain. In fact, there has been a whole host of other compounds developed for just this purpose. For example, there are a variety of other opiates that can relieve the discomfort people feel following an injury. And synthetic morphine-like medications show comparable, and even enhanced, ability to relieve pain. Understanding how the body responds to a painful stimulus has brought us such medications as aspirin, acetaminophen (Tylenol®), and ibuprofen (Motrin®). These medications provide physicians and patients a variety of tools with which to combat pain.

NATURAL MORPHINE-LIKE DRUGS

Natural morphine-like drugs work on the same systems as both opium and morphine. That is, they are opioid agonists. Agonists are hormones, neurotransmitters, or drugs that mimic bodily chemicals. Agonists bind to specific cell receptors in the body, triggering some kind of response. Two common opioid agonists, codeine and thebaine, are both active ingredients of opium. Estimates are that opium contains about 0.5% codeine, 0.2% thebaine, and approximately 10% morphine.

Codeine is a commonly prescribed pain medication, though the analgesia it produces is less than that of morphine (Figure 5.1).

Figure 5.1 Codeine can be derived from opium. It is usually processed into tablets and administered orally. Its ability to relieve pain is less than that of morphine.

Patients can take codeine to manage their pain outside of a hospital setting, as this drug is available in pill form. **Thebaine**, on the other hand, is rarely used in its original form: this compound is usually transformed to other drugs prior to being used for the treatment of pain. Together, these compounds are more commonly used for mild to moderate pain, rather than intense or debilitating pain (for example, a toothache versus post-operative pain).

From these opium-based derivates (morphine, codeine, and thebaine), a whole host of other drugs that are similar in molecular structure can be synthesized. From morphine, we can synthesize heroin, hydromorphone (Dilaudid®), and oxymorphone (Numorphan®), to name a few. From thebaine, we can synthesize oxycodone (Percodan®) and etorphine (Figure 5.2). Regardless of how they are obtained, all these drugs can be used in the treatment of pain.

For example, heroin—believe it or not—is a very effective pain reliever, though only two countries—Canada and the United Kingdom—still employ it for this purpose. Estimates are that heroin, as an analgesic, is approximately three times as potent as morphine. There are several factors that may contribute to its potency. First, heroin undergoes limited first-pass metabolism following its administration (see Chapter 2). This means that, unlike morphine, little of the drug is lost when it is first circulating throughout the body. In addition, heroin also passes rapidly largely unchanged through cellular barriers. Therefore, heroin can enter deep into the brain in its original form, reaching the neuronal pain centers in high concentrations. However, the ease with which heroin bypasses cellular barriers is not always beneficial. Heroin also exits the brain very rapidly, so its analgesic effect is usually short-lived, lasting approximately 4 to 5 hours. When the heroin molecule is metabolized, it is converted from heroin (diacetylmorphine) to morphine. Morphine is then converted to its active and potent metabolite, morphine-6-glucuronide. Thus, the pain relief experienced by people after taking heroin may, in essence, be a combined result of heroin, the morphine molecule, and its metabolite morphine-6-glucuronide.

Hydromorphone, oxymorphone, oxycodone, and etorphine are less effective analgesics than morphine and heroin. Still, they are stronger than codeine in their pain-relieving properties. These drugs are most commonly given in pill

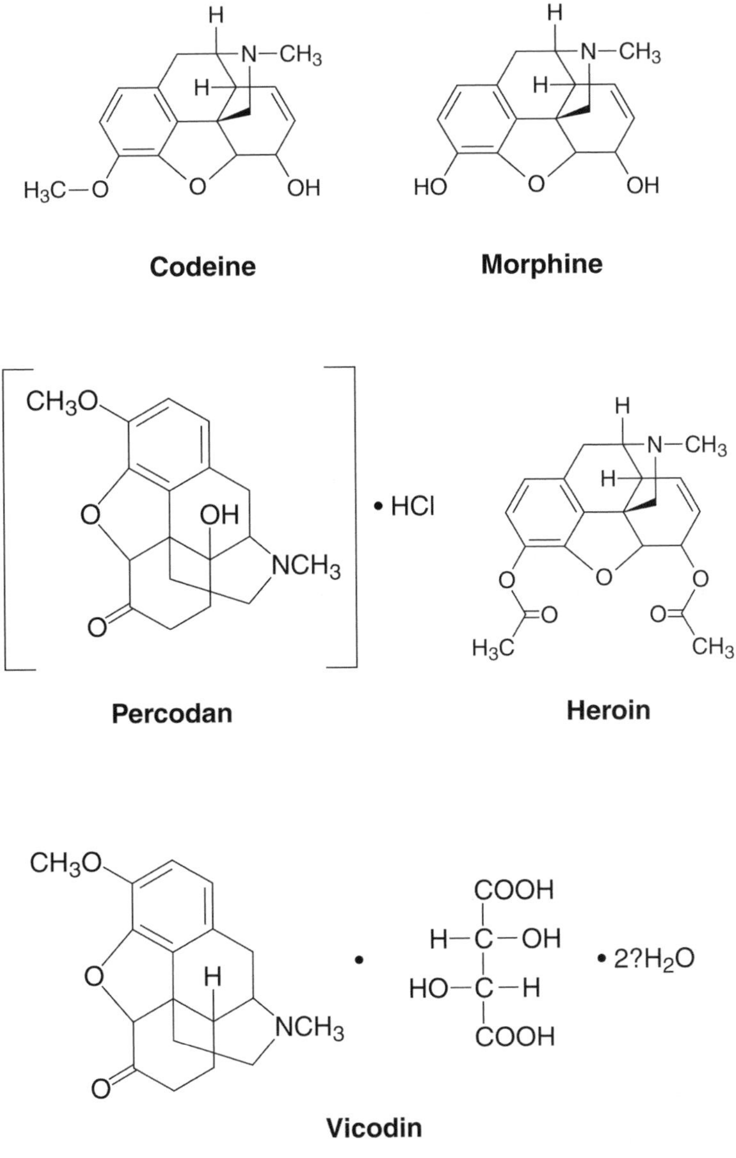

Figure 5.2 The chemical structures of common opiate-based pain medications are all very similar to morphine, though their ability to relieve pain varies.

form, which allows patients to manage their mild to moderate pain themselves.

SYNTHETIC ANALGESICS

In addition to the morphine-like drugs, advances in biochemistry and understanding of the opioid system have led to the development of synthetic analgesics. They work by either directly or indirectly affecting the mu receptor on the opioid neuron, thus modifying opioid activity. The difference between synthetic analgesics and the natural opioid analgesics, however, is that synthetics are not found in nature but, rather, are created from ingredients in the laboratory.

Two prime examples of synthetic analgesics are **meperidine** (Demerol®) and **fentanyl** (Figure 5.3). These drugs were developed in an attempt to synthesize a new pain medication that lacked many of the common side effects that occur with the opiates. It was hoped that the dysphoria, respiratory depression, addiction, and dependence that opiates are notorious for could be avoided if a new compound were tailored with these effects in mind. Unfortunately, this was not the case: following its development, the abuse of meperidine became evident when patients were left to their own devices with the drug. Still, meperidine is an effective weapon against pain, although its potency is only one tenth that of morphine.

Fentanyl and its analogs sufentanil (Sufenta®), alfentanil (Alfenta®), and remifentanil (Ultiva®), on the other hand, are extremely potent analgesics. Estimates are that they are 80 to 500 times more potent than morphine. Their duration of action, however, is rather short-lived, lasting approximately 2 hours. Given how quickly the effects of these drugs dissipate, fentanyl and its analogs are commonly used as an adjunct to anesthesia prior to and after surgery. Still, this drug is very dangerous: fentanyl and fentanyl-like drugs have a high abuse

Figure 5.3 Fentanyl is a synthetic opiate-like pain reliever. It is 80 to 100 times more potent than morphine, but its duration of action is much shorter. Fentanyl (and its analogs) is commonly used to manage post-operative pain.

potential. Even more alarming is that death is more likely with the use of fentanyl and its analogs than with the use of morphine (see "The Siege at a Moscow Theater" box). This is due to their ability to rapidly and profoundly depress breathing. Consequently, these drugs are usually used only under the close supervision of a medical professional.

NONSTEROIDAL ANALGESIC, ANTI-INFLAMMATORY DRUGS

The alternatives to natural and synthetic opioid analgesics are nonsteroidal, anti-inflammatory drugs, or **NSAIDs**. Aspirin, ibuprofen (Advil®, Motrin®), and acetaminophen (Tylenol®) are all considered NSAIDs. The premise behind these medications is to alleviate pain by reducing inflammation at the site of an injury. That is, they work via a peripheral mechanism rather than a central one. NSAIDs reduce the amount of chemicals

THE SIEGE AT A MOSCOW THEATER

On October 23, 2002, 50 Chechen rebels took over the Theater Center on Dubrovka in Moscow, where 800 individuals were taken hostage. The terrorists demanded an end to Russian military action in Chechnya. Although Russian Special Forces responded to this crisis quickly, they did not storm the facility fearing that the explosives that the Chechen rebels had littered throughout the compound would detonate. Over the next 3 days, negotiations with the terrorists yielded no results. Tensions mounted—the hostages were in poor health and fear for their lives finally forced the Russian military to act.

Having experimented with a new opiate-like gas for several years, Russian Special Forces devised a plan to pump this undetectable gas into the theater's ventilation system. It was believed that this gas would incapacitate the terrorists and allow the military to rescue the hostages. On October 25, Russian Special Forces put their plan into action. After administering the gas, they stormed the building and "neutralized" all the terrorists. Unfortunately, 117 hostages also died at the scene. Later, autopsies revealed that the hostages had succumbed to the effects of the gas, being more susceptible due to their poor health. The gas in question was a derivative of fentanyl, a drug that can be fatal when combined with malnutrition, dehydration, and fatigue.

released into the tissue following an injury. As previously noted, these chemicals (such as prostaglandins) are a product of the bruising and swelling that occur after an injury and act to sensitize the pain detector to subsequent stimulation. NSAIDs block the effects of these chemicals and, thus, are very effective at reducing the chronic pain people experience following an injury.

Aspirin is probably the most commonly used NSAID today—estimates are that the public consumes approximately 10,000 to 20,000 tons of aspirin annually. Aspirin is most effective with low-intensity, chronic pain. **Acetaminophen** is a common alternative to aspirin and basically works in a similar fashion. Tylenol is often combined with codeine to increase its pain-relieving potency (this combination of drugs is sold under the trade name Tylenol-4®). It should be noted that chronic acetaminophen use, however, carries the added risk that it can aggravate liver damage caused by other toxins such as alcohol. So, it should be used cautiously in patients who show signs of drug and alcohol abuse. **Ibuprofen** is often better tolerated than aspirin and it is more effective than acetaminophen. In fact, its ability to relieve pain has been equated to that of codeine.

SUMMARY

There are many alternatives to opium and morphine for the treatment of pain. Although some of these drugs may be directly derived from opium and morphine, others are synthesized in a laboratory. There are now pain medications that lessen suffering without any direct effect on the opioid system. These advances have given physicians and patients a variety of tools with which to combat pain.

6

Morphine Addiction and Dependence

Morphine can produce a variety of effects in humans other than pain relief: it can depress breathing and induce vomiting, and cause dizziness, mental clouding, and constipation. One of its more troublesome effects, however, is its addictive properties.

Morphine can precipitate addiction and dependence by interacting with neurons in the brain. Repeated morphine use can actually change the physiological makeup of the body, making someone more prone to becoming addicted and dependent on other substances, such as heroin, cocaine, and alcohol. Thus, one of the key goals of researchers studying the effects of morphine is to understand why this drug results in addiction and dependence. Scientists hope to develop new morphine-like medications that can relieve pain without the potentially addicting side effects of morphine.

MORPHINE USE AND ABUSE

There are important distinctions between morphine use, morphine addiction, and morphine tolerance and dependence (Table 6.1). Specifically, during morphine use, the drug user ingests morphine in a controlled manner and for a specific reason (such as pain relief). There are few to no consequences to the person or his or her family or work. For instance, taking morphine for a limited time to control the pain you feel after having surgery is an acceptable form of morphine use.

Table 6.1 Addiction, Dependence, or Tolerance?

TERM	DEFINITION
Addiction	Physiological or psychological compulsion to participate in a potentially harmful activity, drug, or substance despite the consequences.
Dependence	An uncontrollable need to use a particular substance despite its potentially damaging effects.
Tolerance	The inability of one's body to respond to a drug as a person normally would; usually the result of overexposure to a particular drug or prolonged or abusive use of a chemical substance.

Alternatively, the loss of control over drug-taking is the hallmark feature of morphine addiction. The morphine addict will compulsively ingest the drug at the expense of all other daily activities. For the morphine addict, obtaining the morphine "high" becomes one of the central motivating factors in his or her life. Some addicts will steal from their families, fail to feed their children, or engage in risk-taking behaviors like prostitution just so they can have enough money to get their next "fix."

Morphine tolerance and dependence is a physiological state wherein the individual cannot function appropriately without having the drug in his or her system, sometimes in increasing amounts. If you are dependent on and tolerant to morphine, you may no longer take the drug to get high, but rather to avoid the severe withdrawal symptoms that occur if there is no morphine in your blood. Thus, if a morphine user is not careful with his or her drug intake, controlled morphine use may quickly lead to morphine addiction (out-of-control drug-taking) and, eventually, to morphine tolerance and dependence (the inability to function appropriately unless you have the drug in your system).

BEHAVIORAL FACTORS IN MORPHINE ADDICTION AND DEPENDENCE

One of the reasons that morphine use may lead to morphine addiction is that, following administration, this drug is capable of producing a rewarding sensation. In fact, most substances with abuse potential (such as cocaine, alcohol, and morphine) share this common feature. The rewarding effects of morphine are significant in the context of drug abuse because behaviors followed by a sense of euphoria tend to be repeated. This concept is called **positive reinforcement** and is one of the central features of learning new behaviors. For example, dogs can learn to sit, shake, and roll over by reinforcing those behaviors with tasty dog treats. Similarly, morphine use precipitates subsequent morphine abuse because the ingestion of this drug results in a rewarding sensation, and behaviors that are reinforced tend to increase their likelihood.

When a person becomes tolerant to and dependent on morphine, they may no longer actively seek out morphine reward, but rather avoid morphine **withdrawal**. Morphine withdrawal symptoms are, for the most part, opposite to those effects that occur when an individual is on morphine. For instance, when taking morphine, a person will feel no pain and there will be a sense of euphoria as well as the occurrence of constipation and sedation. People going through morphine withdrawal often report the opposite: they describe a sense of pain and itching, dysphoria (a sick feeling), severe diarrhea, and an inability to sleep. Thus, a robust rebound effect occurs when a morphine-dependent person stops taking morphine and goes into withdrawal.

Together, these symptoms are very unpleasant and punishing, an effect that may either: (a) motivate someone to begin using morphine again, or (b) cause an individual to increase the dose of morphine he or she uses. In the context of learning, these phenomena are called punishment and negative reinforcement. Behaviors (such as the act of physically stopping morphine use) tend to decrease in likelihood if they result in punishment (withdrawal symptoms). Alternatively, behaviors that result in the removal of punishment, such as taking more morphine to avoid withdrawal, tend to increase in likelihood. This concept is called **negative reinforcement**. Together, drug-taking in a morphine-dependent individual is fueled by the potential that cessation of morphine use will result in withdrawal, as well as by the realization that morphine withdrawal can be avoided by continued and escalated drug use.

THE BIOLOGICAL BASES OF MORPHINE ADDICTION

Similar to morphine's ability to relieve pain, morphine produces a rewarding feeling through its interaction with neurons in the brain. There are certain groups of neurons within the brain that are responsible for mediating the rewarding sensations of reinforcing stimuli, like morphine. It is important to note, however, that the reward systems of the brain are not only activated by drugs like morphine, but by any activity that feels good such as eating or laughing.

The neuronal systems responsible for reward are located within the midbrain and forebrain. These structures (or clusters of neurons) are called the **ventral tegmental area (VTA)**, the **nucleus accumbens**, and the **medial prefrontal cortex** (Figure 6.1). These structures are able to communicate with one another because they all share several common features.

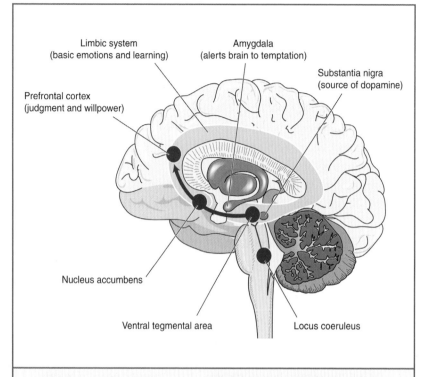

Figure 6.1 The major brain centers that mediate the rewarding sensation of drugs: the ventral tegmental area (VTA), the nucleus accumbens, and the medial prefrontal cortex. The major neurotransmitter released by the neurons in these centers is dopamine.

These structures send direct axonal projections to one another, so that only small synaptic spaces exist between them. The VTA, nucleus accumbens, and medial prefrontal cortex all use the same neurotransmitters to communicate with one another. These neurotransmitters are dopamine and glutamate, though it is generally accepted that **dopamine** is the major player in drug reward.

When you partake in an activity that generally feels good, VTA neurons become active and release dopamine onto the dopamine receptors in the nucleus accumbens. In addition, there is also the release of dopamine and glutamate from the VTA to neurons in the medial prefrontal cortex, which, in turn, releases more glutamate back onto the neurons of the nucleus accumbens. The net result of this activity is an activation of the nucleus accumbens. This neuronal activity produces pleasant sensations that motivate an individual to repeat and learn new behaviors. This system is in place to teach people about the value of behaviors like eating, drinking, or propagating the species. Unfortunately, it can also be hijacked by drugs like morphine.

Morphine produces a sense of euphoria because it causes the brain's reward system to become active when it should not be. Morphine accomplishes this feat by indirectly boosting levels of dopamine (and glutamate) around the VTA, nucleus accumbens, and medial prefrontal cortex (Figure 6.2). That is, although morphine does not directly cause the neurons within the VTA to become active and release dopamine (and glutamate), it does have effects on other neurons around the VTA with opioid receptors (mainly the mu receptor) on them. Specifically, opioid neurons synapse onto the inhibitory interneurons. These inhibitory interneurons directly communicate with the VTA, functioning to lessen (or regulate) the everyday natural release of dopamine within the brain's reward system. In other words, the inhibitory interneurons modulate and tone down the reward response.

When opioid neurons are active, they display an inhibitory action on neuronal communication—they stop neurons from communicating with one another. In the context of the brain's reward system, opioid neurons stop inhibitory interneurons from communicating with neurons in the VTA. This activity results in a phenomenon called disinhibition (the inability to suppress impulsive behavior and emotions). Thus, when morphine is present in the human system, dopamine and glutamate levels in the VTA rise and the nucleus accumbens becomes active. With the activation

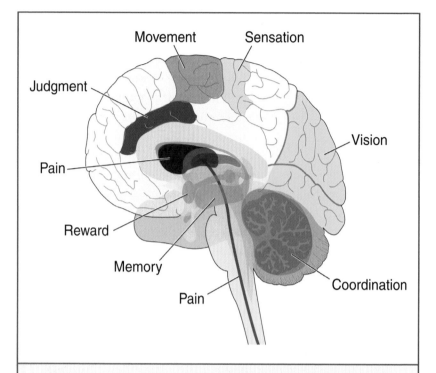

Figure 6.2 This diagram depicts where opiates act to affect the major brain centers that mediate the rewarding sensation of drugs. Opiates alter the communication between neurons in the ventral tegmental area (VTA) and the nucleus accumbens. This modulation, however, is not direct. That is, opiates inhibit input to these sites, boosting the level of dopamine released by the VTA and the nucleus accumbens.

of the nucleus accumbens, the morphine user feels a sense of reward and the act of taking morphine is reinforced.

CAUSES OF MORPHINE TOLERANCE AND DEPENDENCE

Morphine dependence is mediated by mechanisms that are different from, yet related to, those involved in morphine addiction. In fact, there are several biological avenues that can lead to the emergence of morphine dependence following the onset of morphine addiction. For example, when a person repeatedly takes morphine, as in the case of morphine abuse, his or her brain responds to the continuous presence of the drug by desensitizing itself to the effects of the drug, and **neuronal tolerance** ensues. Therefore, the amount of morphine that an addict usually takes no longer produces the same effect as it once did.

Neuronal tolerance to morphine occurs at the level of the dendritic receptor. Neurons respond to repeated morphine-induced activation by reducing (down-regulating) the number of dendritic mu receptors that morphine can attach to (Figure 6.3). This down-regulation occurs through a process called internalization: dendritic mu receptors leave the surface of the dendrites and move into the neuron so that the drug molecule is incapable of attaching to the receptor. Thus, although morphine levels in the blood and brain remain unchanged, morphine is no longer capable of activating opioid neurons as it did before.

Neuronal tolerance can also explain why there is a tendency for morphine addicts to increase their daily dosage with continued morphine use and it provides an explanation for why morphine withdrawal occurs once morphine use has stopped. When neurons with opioid receptors on them become desensitized to the effects of morphine, morphine users will no longer get high when taking the same dose of morphine. So, they increase their dose to counteract the desensitization of their opioid neurons.

In addition, these neurons actually become less active than they normally would be if a morphine-dependent person fails to take their daily dose of the drug. That is, tolerant opioid neurons will only function normally while in the presence of the morphine. It is generally believed that this toned down neuronal activity accounts for the rebound effects (pain, itching, and diarrhea) evident during morphine withdrawal. Therefore, as morphine addicts continue to take the drug, they

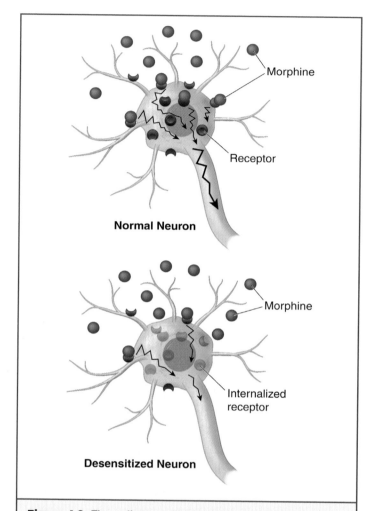

Figure 6.3 These diagrams illustrate the normal activity of a neuron when activated by morphine (top panel), and the activity of a neuron that is tolerant to the effects of morphine (bottom panel). The differences between the two are that the morphine-tolerant neuron has internalized some of its mu receptors, thus, lessening the effects that morphine can produce.

incrementally increase their dose to either regain their high or achieve normalcy. Unfortunately, such an activity usually results in greater tolerance and dependence.

7

Heroin Abuse

The abuse of morphine is no longer as common an occurrence as it was in the 19th century. Although there are probably multiple reasons why morphine abuse has declined, one particular factor may have contributed to this phenomenon more than the others—the availability and use of heroin may have replaced people's propensity to abuse morphine. Supporting this assumption is the fact that heroin is a relatively cheap drug, one that is readily available on the streets of most cities, suburbs, and towns. Heroin has been said to produce a high that is more intense than the high that occurs with morphine injections. Thus, over time, addicts probably shifted their preference away from morphine to heroin.

THE HISTORY OF HEROIN

In 1874, British chemist C. R. Wright discovered a new derivative of morphine by boiling morphine over a hot stove. This process essentially resulted in the acetylization of the morphine molecule to form diacetylmorphine, commonly known as **heroin**. Through experimentation, it was found that this new drug was far more potent than morphine in many of its effects, such as pain relief and cough suppression. Given its efficacy, the Bayer Pharmaceutical Company began mass production of heroin in 1898 and marketed it as a treatment for chronic coughs and asthma (Figure 7.1).

As in the case of opium and morphine, however, chronic consumption of this drug resulted in an epidemic of addiction and dependence among its users. As a result, tough legislation was

Figure 7.1 This advertisement was distributed by the Bayer Pharmaceutical Company for heroin, which was marketed as a cough suppressant.

enacted to curb its use. Although the banning of heroin resulted in a brief decline of its use in the 1930s, drug traffickers soon realized the value of this drug and a black market for heroin emerged, which continues to this day.

Today, heroin is recognized as one of the most addictive and dangerous known drugs. Given the limited legal production of heroin that occurs today, this drug is most commonly obtained from illicit opium (see Chapter 1) that has found its way to clandestine laboratories around the world. This "street" heroin can come in many different forms. Heroin is commonly sold on the street as either a white or brown powder (Figure 7.2) and it may also come as a black, tarry residue, called "black-tar heroin." Other common street names for heroin include "junk," "H," "skag," and "smack."

The purity of heroin varies greatly depending on where, when, and from whom it was purchased. It is common for heroin dealers to "cut" their product to maximize their profits. Cutting heroin involves diluting the purity of the drug, often with other substances like sugar, starch, powdered milk, quinine, or strychnine (rat poison). Thus, illicit heroin purchasers never know what exactly they are taking when heroin is bought on the street.

In 1998, the lifetime prevalence of heroin use among people in the United States was estimated at 2.4 million individuals. The majority of these users were over 30 years of age. However, there has also been a recent upswing in younger people using heroin. Government surveys indicate that about 1.5% of 8th, 10th, and 12th graders have used heroin at some point in their lifetime (Table 7.1). Such statistics are alarming given the death rate that is associated with heroin use (from strokes and other health problems).

HEROIN USE

The most common way that people administer heroin is by intravenous injection (Figure 7.3). Since heroin is usually

Figure 7.2 Heroin is usually sold as a white or brown powder. However, it may also come as a black, tarry residue, called "black-tar heroin."

sold as a powder, the heroin addict usually makes the drug injectable by dissolving this powder into a liquid through a crude cooking process. Most heroin addicts will take the drug at least four times a day.

Heroin users do not always inject the drug into the veins of their arms. One reason that alternative injection sites are used is that heroin users are most often identifiable by the marks on their arms from previous injections, their "track" marks. Many heroin abusers try to hide this telltale sign from their friends, families, coworkers, and especially the law by injecting the drug in other places on their body.

In recent times, snorting and smoking heroin have become popular methods of administration among the heroin-using population. Although both these methods produce a high that is described as less than the one produced by the injection

Table 7.1 Heroin Use by Students, 2004: Monitoring the Future (MTF) Survey

	8th-GRADERS	10th-GRADERS	12th-GRADERS
Lifetime	1.6%	1.5%	1.5%
Annual	1.0	0.9	0.9
30-Day	0.5	0.5	0.5

From http://www.nida.nih.gov/PDF/Infofacts/Heroin05.pdf.

* "Lifetime" refers to use at least once during a respondent's lifetime. "Annual" refers to an individual's drug use at least once during the year preceding their response to the survey. "30-day" refers to an individual's drug use at least once during the month preceding their response to the survey.

of heroin, these methods provide the heroin user with an alternative way to hide his or her drug use.

THE EFFECTS OF HEROIN

If heroin is injected, the effects of the drug occur almost immediately (within 7 to 8 minutes). A similar rapid effect occurs if heroin is smoked, but not if it is snorted. Most often, the effects of heroin last from 4 to 5 hours.

Heroin users report a "rush" immediately after the drug is administered (Table 7.2). Accompanying this rush is dry mouth and a flushing of the skin. Mental clouding will then soon set in and the heroin user falls into a dream-like state, commonly referred to as "the nod." Heroin users often state that they

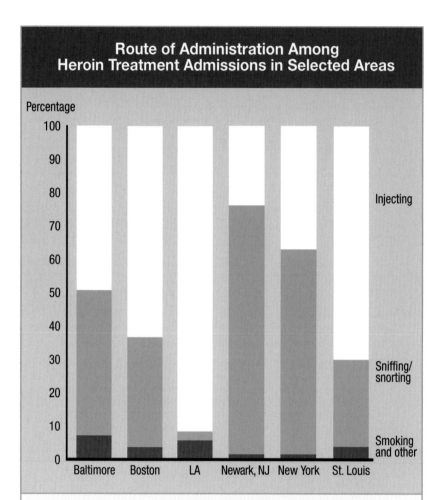

Figure 7.3 Heroin users commonly inject their heroin intravenously, though snorting and smoking heroin is on the rise. The chart shows the percentage of users in six major cities that participate primarily in the different forms of heroin drugs abuse. The white bar shows the amount of users who inject the drug, the light blue represents those who sniff or snort it, and the dark blue represents those who smoke heroin or use some other method of administration.

became nauseous with their first heroin "fix," but, given the euphoric feeling that accompanies heroin administration, they describe this effect as a "good sick."

Table 7.2 Short-Term and Long-Term Effects of Heroin Use

SHORT-TERM EFFECTS	LONG-TERM EFFECTS
"Rush"	Addiction
Depressed respiration	Infectious diseases, for example, HIV/AIDS and hepatitis B and C
Clouded mental functioning	Collapsed veins
Nausea and vomiting	Bacterial infections
Suppression of pain	Abscesses
Spontaneous abortion	Infection of heart lining and valves
	Arthritis and other rheumatologic problems

From http://www.nida.nih.gov/ResearchReports/Heroin/heroin3.html#long.

The effects of using heroin are not always short-lived. Because addicts commonly administer heroin multiple times a day, every day of the week, many changes to the body can occur with continued heroin abuse. For instance, veins in the arms often collapse because of the trauma of repetitive injections. Heroin addicts refer to collapsed veins as veins that are "burned out." Further, multiple abscesses (infections) on the arms at previous sites of injection (referred to as being "bugged"), as well as other infections of the heart and soft tissues, are common in heroin addicts. As previously noted, clogging of the veins and arteries by the impurities mixed in with the heroin may also occur. Blocking blood flow by these means may lead to localized cell death, heart attacks, and even strokes.

HEROIN USE AND HIV/AIDS

One of the more troubling consequences of intravenous heroin use is the likelihood that a user will contract **human immuno-deficiency virus (HIV)**, the cause of acquired immune deficiency syndrome (AIDS). In fact, injection drug use is responsible for a third of all HIV cases in the United States. For the heroin-injecting population, the most common means of transmission is through the sharing of needles. It is common for heroin users to gather in large groups in abandoned homes called "shooting galleries" (a term coined by the writer William S. Burroughs, who often wrote frankly about his own drug addiction) and share heroin together.

HIV is a virus that lives in the blood; injection-drug users introduce heroin into blood circulation via hypodermic needles—sharing non-sterile needles acts as a vector for the transmission of the disease among this population. Sharing needles at shooting galleries presents the possibility that one HIV-infected heroin user could transmit the disease to 10 or 20 other individuals. It should be noted that heroin users also engage in other risk-taking behaviors (such as prostitution and unprotected sex) at a greater rate than the non-drug-using population. Transmission of HIV may occur in these ways, as well.

SUMMARY

Heroin, like the other opiates before it, was thrust onto the public as a "wonder drug" capable of lessening the suffering of people. Over time, however, its negative effects began to outweigh its benefits. Although tough legislation was enacted to curb the heroin use problem, this drug found a foothold in society, where it remains a significant social and public health issue to this day.

8

Treatment of Opiate Addiction and Dependence

For most opiate addicts, breaking the cycle of opiate abuse (sometimes referred to as "kicking the habit") requires a strong desire to stop using drugs. In addition to realizing that withdrawal will inevitably ensue following the cessation of opiate use, most opiate addicts know that they will face many psychological hurdles during and after their recovery. Opiate addicts must re-learn how to live life without taking drugs, and for this reason, clinicians and scientists have intensely sought effective treatments to aid opiate addicts on their road to recovery.

OPIATE DETOXIFICATION AND RELAPSE

Prior to the advent of opiate antagonist and substitution therapies (discussed later in this chapter), the only options for quitting opiate use was to either sequentially reduce the dose of the abused opiate taken over some specified period of time (taper the dose) or to go cold turkey (abruptly stop drug use completely). The term *cold turkey* was derived from the fact that opiate addicts going through withdrawal often become cold and clammy to the touch and develop goose bumps, an appearance much like an uncooked turkey. This process of stopping drug abuse is called **detoxification**. Unfortunately, such methods are only effective for a small percentage of people. Individuals who attempt to cease opiate use only by means of detoxification are at significant risk for a relapse. In the context of drug abuse and dependence, **relapse** is defined as the resumption of full-blown drug use after a period of not using the drug at all (abstinence).

Several mechanisms have recently been postulated to account for the occurrence of relapse in the drug-addicted population. In the addict, exposure to several types of stimuli may trigger the resumption of full-blown drug use, including environmental cues, re-exposure to drugs, or an experience of stress. Environmental cues trigger relapse by reminding the opiate addict of a period in life when he or she was using drugs. These cues can include, among other things, watching a scene in a movie where heroin is being used or smelling an odor reminiscent of a shooting gallery. These cues and memories may result in the indirect activation of brain areas, such as the ventral tegmental area, nucleus accumbens, and medial prefrontal cortex (see Chapter 6), areas linked to drug-craving and drug-seeking.

Exposure to drugs, on the other hand, triggers relapse because drug addicts are said to be biologically sensitized to the effects of drugs. In this context, sensitization refers to the fact that the physical makeup of the brain has changed throughout the course of addiction, where exposure to a previously ineffective quantity of drug causes activation in the brain's reward system. The drug user now experiences a sense of euphoria with a limited dose of drug: just a taste of drug will precipitate an occurrence of relapse in the addict. Even more troublesome is the fact that the drug "trigger" need not be the same drug that was previously abused. The rates of relapse are higher in opiate addicts who continue to use other drugs, such as alcohol or cocaine, than in addicts who cease their drug use altogether.

Finally, having a stressful experience may also cause an opiate addict to relapse. Often, addicts had used opiates as a coping mechanism for the stresses of everyday life, for example, while working at a job they did not like or dealing with a bad-tempered child. Thus, the ex-opiate addict may resume his or her drug use to cope with a bad day.

MEDICATIONS FOR THE
PREVENTION OF OPIATE RELAPSE

The potential to relapse poses a significant problem to an opiate addict attempting to stop their his or her habit. Scientists have developed medications that aid in the prevention of relapse. Two compounds, naltrexone (Trexan®, Revia®) and naloxone (Narcan®), have shown promise as anti-relapse medications (Figure 8.1). These drugs are considered synthetic mu opioid receptor antagonists. An antagonist is a compound that attaches to the dendritic receptor of a neuron, but has no effect on its own (Figure 8.2). Antagonists prevent agonists (like opioid neurotransmitters or opiate drugs) from also attaching to the neuronal dendritic receptor. Thus, when agonists are in the presence of antagonists, there will be no neuronal activation. Given that naltrexone and naloxone are mu receptor antagonists, they inhibit the ability of opiates, like morphine or heroin, from producing neuronal activation at the mu receptor and, thus, euphoria. The net result of this activity is a blockade of opiate reward, an effect that essentially reduces the value of opiates to the addict.

Although using these compounds seems ideal for preventing opiate relapse, there are several factors that limit their effectiveness. Naloxone cannot be given by mouth because this drug will undergo extensive metabolism (first-pass metabolism) before it reaches the brain centers involved in drug reward. It is therefore mainly used as a tool to resuscitate patients who have overdosed on heroin—in the hospital, they are given naloxone intravenously to reverse the effects of heroin.

Naltrexone is effective when administered orally and its ability to block the rewarding properties of opiates can last up

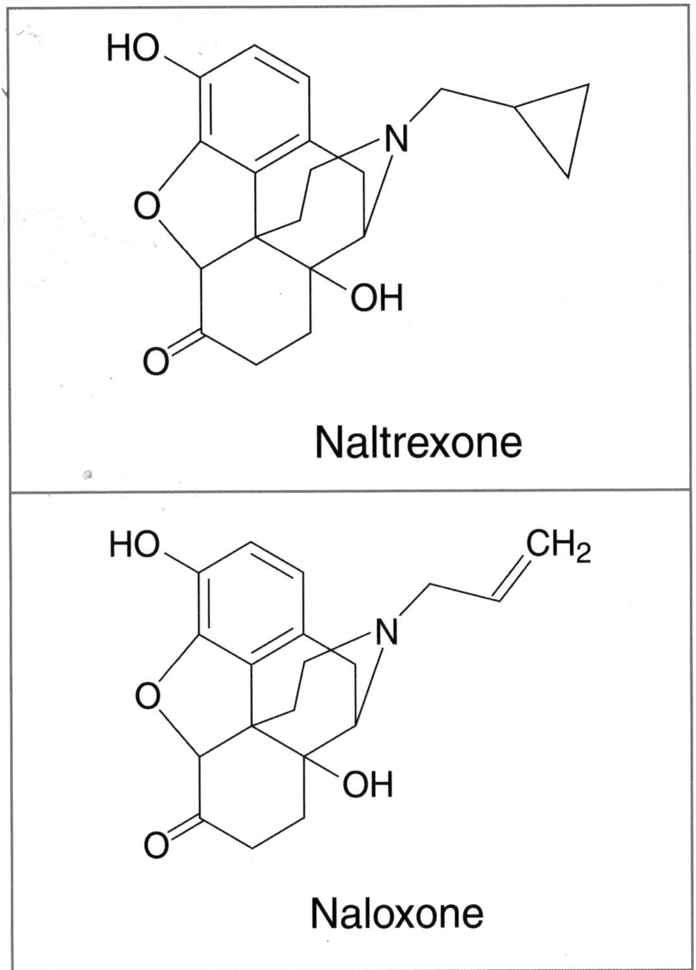

Figure 8.1 Top: Naltrexone can prevent the occurrence of relapse in opiate addicts. It is an antagonist at the opioid receptor, blocking the effects of opiates at the mu receptor. Bottom: Naloxone is an effective anti-relapse medication, though it is primarily used to treat victims of heroin overdoses. Like naltrexone, it is an antagonist at the mu receptor.

to 3 days. These factors allow opiate addicts to administer naltrexone outside of a hospital setting and at intervals that do not interfere with their everyday lives. The limiting factor

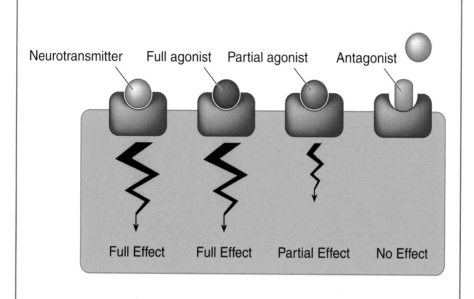

Figure 8.2 The relative effects of neurotransmitters, as well as drug agonists, partial agonists, and antagonists at the neuronal receptor. Antagonists have no effect on their own when attached to a neuronal receptor; they work by preventing agonists from attaching to the receptor.

with using naltrexone is that, with opiate addicts, patient compliance with taking this medication is low. One reason for low compliance is that addicts often report that naltrexone produces a dysphoric (aversive and punishing) feeling. Thus, opiate addicts avoid taking this drug because it makes them feel sick. This is consistent with learning theory in that activities that result in punishment tend to decrease in likelihood (see Chapter 6).

So, although these medications are effective at preventing opiate reward and the potential for relapse, their practicality for the treatment of addiction is somewhat limited.

SUBSTITUTION THERAPIES

Another approach to dealing with opiate addiction involves stabilization rather than complete detoxification from opiates. Some argue that the problem with abusing drugs is not the use of the drug per se, but rather the psychological, medical, social, and legal consequences that go hand-in-hand with compulsive drug-taking. For example, activities like theft and prostitution are intimately linked to the search for drugs by addicts that can neither afford nor find their next fix. Further, the health consequences of intravenous drug use (such as the spread of HIV/AIDS) results from the sharing of needles rather than from the effects of the drug. Thus, many believe that the answer to treating opiate addiction is to stabilize drug use rather than to eliminate it. This is the rationale for opiate substitution therapies.

The employment of **methadone** and **LAAM (levo-alpha-acetylmethadol-hydrochloride)** are the most traditional substitution therapies for opiate addiction (Figure 8.3). Methadone was developed in Germany during World War II, whereas LAAM was synthesized in the 1970s. These compounds are semi-synthetic mu opioid receptor agonists that produce only a small degree of analgesia and euphoria. So, although these drugs have the same biological action as the abused opiates, they do not produce the same level of euphoria that occurs with morphine or heroin. Their ability to produce only a moderate level of euphoria is an important factor in their utility as substitution therapies. These drugs are also effective for up to 72 hours when administered by mouth (methadone lasts 24 hours, while LAAM lasts for up to 72 hours). Their long duration of action aids in the reduction of opiate cravings and, it is hoped, the search for opiates on the street.

Although methadone and LAAM are effective when administered orally, these drugs are usually not given to a patient to take home. Rather, they are dispensed and taken at

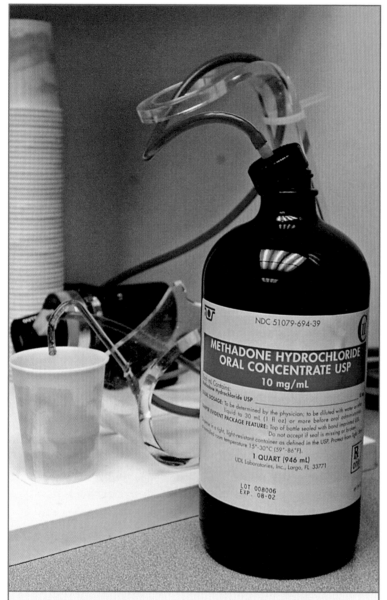

Figure 8.3 Methadone is commonly used as a substitution therapy for opiate abuse. The premise behind using methadone is to lessen the addict's craving for opiates and, thus, the problem behaviors associated with opiate abuse.

methadone clinics. There are several reasons for administering methadone and LAAM in a clinical setting. First, when left on their own, opiate addicts are notorious for taking more than their allotted dose of methadone or LAAM. Although the euphoria produced by these drugs is less than that which occurs with morphine or heroin, frequent high-dose administration of these compounds can give the user a greater sense of euphoria. Using substitution drugs in this manner defeats the whole purpose of the therapy. Second, opiate addicts may actually sell their methadone or LAAM to other opiate addicts in order to buy heroin, which, again, defeats the purpose of the therapy. The U. S. government has mandated that the administration of methadone be done in clinics under the close supervision of health-care professionals, though, recently, LAAM has received approval to be taken home.

More recently, a drug named buprenorphine has been introduced as a substitution therapy for opiate addiction. **Buprenorphine** is a semi-synthetic opiate that is derived from thebaine. Unlike methadone and LAAM, which are pure agonists, buprenorphine is a partial agonist for the mu receptor. Partial agonists are drugs that have both agonistic and antagonistic properties at a single neuronal receptor. Thus, a partial agonist will produce less of an effect, like euphoria, than a drug that is pure agonist. Still, recent reports have suggested that buprenorphine is abused. For this reason, some clinicians now combine both buprenorphine and naloxone in an attempt to decrease the likelihood of buprenorphine abuse.

NEEDLE-EXCHANGE PROGRAMS

Many metropolitan areas use needle-exchange programs to help the opiate addict stay healthy (Figure 8.4). Needle exchange programs are not meant to cure opiate addiction. Rather, their intention is to prevent the spread of infectious diseases such as AIDS and hepatitis among intravenous drug users.

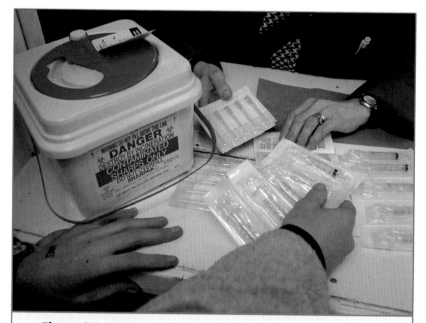

Figure 8.4 Needle-exchange programs are used to decrease the spread of diseases such as AIDS among the intravenous drug-using population. These programs have been met with resistance by communities that wish to rid themselves of the drug problem.

In other words, they are harm-reduction programs. Since the spread of diseases is related to the sharing of dirty needles among heroin users, it makes sense that the transmission of such diseases can be lessened if addicts have access to sterile drug paraphernalia.

Although there is a general lack of scientific data regarding the outcomes of these programs, anecdotal evidence suggests that they are effective at reducing disease transmission. Opponents, however, argue that such programs encourage continued opiate abuse rather than provide a treatment option for the drug user. Thus, needle-exchange programs have been met with stiff opposition by communities that wish to rid themselves of the drug problem plaguing their neighborhoods (see "Switzerland's Needle Park" box).

SUMMARY

Opiate drugs such as morphine are, by far, the most effective substances we have to combat pain. Unfortunately, using these drugs comes with a price: those who use opiates for long periods of time are at significant risk for becoming addicted and dependent on these drugs. Understanding how these drugs work within the body will provide the key to combating pain without these added risks. And new treatments for opiate addiction provide a glimmer of hope for the opiate addict who wishes to quit his or her habit. Regardless, history has taught us that these drugs will continue to be used and abused for years to come.

SWITZERLAND'S NEEDLE PARK

In the 1990s, the Swiss government devised a new program to deal with the heroin problem plaguing its country. Under the belief that heroin users would continue to use drugs despite community outreach and treatment programs, the Swiss government decided to provide heroin users with a centralized safe haven where they could sell and use their drugs. With this program, the government for the first time would be able to reach most of the heroin-using population, providing them with clean needles and health care. The hope was that the widespread crime, prostitution, and the spread of disease that goes hand-in-hand with heroin use would decrease as more heroin addicts showed up at this location known as Needle Park.

Initially, the program was quite a success: crime was down and the spread of disease was under control. Soon, however, addicts from all over Europe learned that such a place existed. The number of heroin addicts visiting Needle Park grew exponentially and drug use, crime, and disease spilled out into the surrounding community. The government had no choice but to close down the program.

Glossary

Acetaminophen—A commonly prescribed nonsteroidal, anti-inflammatory drug, or NSAID.

Analgesic—Pain reliever.

Association cortex—An area of the brain that perceives the locale of pain experienced.

Axons—Branch-like protrusions that originate from the cell body of the neuron and are chiefly responsible for sending signals to other neurons.

Buprenorphine—A semi-synthetic opiate derived from thebaine that is used as a substitution therapy for opiate addiction.

Central nervous system—The brain and spinal cord.

Codeine—A commonly prescribed pain medication obtained from the poppy plant.

Dendrites—Tubular branch-like protrusions that emanate from neurons and are responsible for receiving signals from other neurons.

Detoxification—The process of stopping drug abuse.

Dopamine—The major neurotransmitter in the reward systems of the brain.

Dynorphin—A naturally occurring opioid peptide.

Dysphoric—Aversive.

Endorphin—A naturally occurring opioid peptide.

Enkephalin—A naturally occurring opioid peptide.

Euphoria—A sense of well-being.

Fentanyl—A synthetic analgesic; its analogs are sufentanil (Sufenta®), alfentanil (Alfenta®), and remifentanyl (Ultiva®).

Glutamate—A neurotransmitter involved in the perception of pain (and reward).

Heroin—Diacetylmorphine, a more potent derivative of morphine. It is recognized as one of the most addictive and dangerous drugs known. Common street names for heroin include "junk," "H," "skag," and "smack."

Human immunodeficiency virus (HIV)—The virus that causes acquired immune deficiency syndrome (AIDS).

Ibuprofen—A commonly prescribed nonsteroidal, anti-inflammatory drug, or NSAID.

LAAM (levo-alpha-acetylmethadol-hydrochloride)—A substitution therapy for opiate addiction; a semi-synthetic mu opioid receptor agonist that produces only a small degree of analgesia and euphoria.

Laudanum—Opium mixed with wine and spices.

Medial prefrontal cortex—Neuronal system, located within the forebrain, responsible for reward. It works in concert with the ventral tegmental area (VTA) and the nucleus accumbens.

Meperidine—A synthetic analgesic (trade name Demerol®).

Metabolic sensitization—Drug levels rise in the blood as the body loses its ability to break down the compound. This produces a stronger drug effect than occurred with the same dose of drug previously.

Metabolite—A byproduct of drug breakdown.

Metabolize—Break down.

Methadone—A substitution therapy for opiate addiction; a semi-synthetic mu opioid receptor agonist that produces only a small degree of analgesia and euphoria.

Morphine-6-glucuronide—An active metabolite of morphine.

Negative reinforcement—Behaviors that result in the removal of punishment, such as taking more morphine to avoid withdrawal symptoms, tend to increase in likelihood.

Neuronal tolerance—The amount of a drug no longer produces the same effect as it once did.

Neurons—Specialized cells that give people the ability to sense and perceive things, experience emotions, think, and produce coordinated movement. They are found in great abundance in the brain and spinal cord (the central nervous system), as well as in and around muscles, organs, and tissues (the peripheral nervous system).

Neurotransmitters—Chemical messengers that facilitate the communication between neurons.

Nociceptive nerve pathways—Neuronal systems that deal with the sensation and perception of pain.

NSAIDs—Nonsteroidal, anti-inflammatory drugs.

Nucleus accumbens—Neuronal system, located within the midbrain forebrain, responsible for reward. It works in concert with the ventral tegmental area (VTA) and the medial prefrontal cortex.

Glossary

Opiates—A family of drugs, including morphine and heroin, obtained from the poppy plant known for producing a wide range of effects, from sedation to constipation, but most commonly used for the management of pain.

Opioid agonist—A drug that mimics the effects of the opioid peptides.

Opioid system—Group of neurons that have certain types of receptors on them, called opioid receptors. Morphine works by affecting these receptors.

Opium—A naturally occurring drug that is cultivated from the poppy plant, *Papaver somniferum*. Morphine is one of the principal ingredients of opium.

Peripheral nervous system—The nerves and neurons outside the central nervous system in and around muscles, organs, and tissues.

Poppy—The plant, *Papaver somniferum*, from which opium is harvested. Only four countries—Australia, France, Spain, and Turkey—legitimately grow poppy plant crops for medicinal use.

Positive reinforcement—Behaviors followed by a sense of euphoria tend to be repeated. It is one of the central features of learning new behaviors, including drug adiction.

Precept—A mental representation of the external environment.

Relapse—The resumption of full-blown drug use after a period of not using the drug at all (abstinence).

Route of administration—The method of introducing a drug into the body.

Somatosensory cortex—An area of the brain that perceives the type of pain experienced.

Substance P—A neurotransmitter involved in the perception of pain.

Synapse—The microscopic gap between neurons.

Thalamus—An area of the brain considered the gatekeeper for most information entering the higher areas of the cortex.

Thebaine—A medication obtained from the poppy plant that is usually transformed to other drugs prior to being used for the treatment of pain.

Ventral tegmental area (VTA)—Neuronal system, located within the midbrain, responsible for reward. It works in concert with the nucleus accumbens and the medial prefrontal cortex.

Withdrawal—The symptoms experienced when a person stops taking a drug.

Bibliography

Booth, M. *Opium: A History.* New York: St. Martin's Griffin, 1996.

Brownstein, M. J. "A Brief History of Opiates, Opioid Peptides, and Opioid Receptors." *Proceedings of the National Academy of Sciences* 15 (1993): 5931–5933.

Contet, C., B. L. Kieffer, and K. Befort. "Mu Opioid Receptor: A Gateway to Drug Addiction." *Current Opinions in Neurobiology* 14 (2004): 370–378.

de Quincy, Thomas. *Confessions of an English Opium Eater.* New York: J. T. Little and Ives, 1932.

Dole, V. P. "Implications of Methadone Maintenance for Theories of Narcotic Addiction." *Journal of the American Medical Association* 260 (1988): 3025–3029.

Edmeads, J. "The Physiology of Pain: A Review." *Progress in Neuropsychopharmacology and Biological Psychiatry* 7 (1983): 413–419.

Feldman, R. S., J. S. Meyer, and L. F. Quenzer. "Peptide Neurotransmitters." In Feldman, R. S., J. S. Meyer, and L.F. Quenzer (eds.). *Principles of Neuropsychopharmacology.* Sunderland, MA: Sinauer Associates, 1997, pp. 455–548.

Goldstein, A. "Heroin, Morphine, and Other Opiates." In Goldstein, A. (ed.). *Addiction: From Biology to Drug Policy,* 2nd ed. New York: Oxford University Press, 2001, pp. 157–177.

Hodgson, B. *In the Arms of Morpheus: The Tragic History of Laudanum, Morphine, and Patent Medicines.* Buffalo, NY: Firefly Books, 2001.

Hodgson, B. *Opium: A Portrait of a Heavenly Demon.* San Francisco: Chronicle Books, 1999.

Julien, R. M. "Nonnarcotic, Anti-inflamatory Analgesics." In Julien, R. M. (ed.). *A Primer for Drug Action: A Concise Nontechnical Guide to the Actions, Uses, and Side Effects of Psychoactive Drugs,* 9th ed. New York: Worth Publishers, 2001, pp. 287–298.

Julien, R. M. "Opioid Analgesics." In Julien, R. M. (ed.). *A Primer for Drug Action: A Concise Nontechnical Guide to the Actions, Uses, and Side Effects of Psychoactive Drugs,* 9th ed. New York: Worth Publishers, 2001, pp. 250–286.

Bibliography

Julien, R. M. "Pharmacokinetics: How Drugs are Handled by the Body." In Julien, R. M. (ed.). *A Primer for Drug Action: A Concise Nontechnical Guide to the Actions, Uses, and Side Effects of Psychoactive Drugs*, 9th ed. New York: Worth Publishers, 2001, pp. 2–36.

Kandel, E. R., J. H. Schwartz, and T. M. Jessel. "Pain and Analgesia." In Kandel, E. R., J. H. Schwartz, and T. M. Jessel (eds.). *Principles of Neural Science*, 3rd ed. New York: Elsevier Science Publishing, 1991, pp. 385–399.

Koob, G. F. "Drugs of Abuse—Anatomy, Pharmacology and Function of Reward Pathways." *Trends in Pharmacological Research* 13 (1992): 177–184.

Kreek, M. J. and F. J. Vocci. "History and Current Status of Opioid Maintenance Treatments: Blending Conference Session." *Journal of Substance Abuse and Treatment* 23 (2002): 93–105.

Levinthal, C. F. "The Major Narcotics: Opium, Morphine and Heroin." In Levinthal, C. F. (ed.). *Drugs, Behavior and Modern Society*, 3rd ed. Boston: Allyn & Bacon, 2002, pp. 100–123.

Lotsch, J. and G. Geisslinger. "Morphine-6-Glucuronide: An Analgesic of the Future?" *Clinical Pharmacokinetics* 40 (2001): 485–499.

Lugo, R. A. and S. E. Kern. "Clinical Pharmacokinetics of Morphine." *Journal of Pain, Palliative Care and Pharmacotherapy* 16 (2002): 5–18.

Miller, R. J. and P. B. Tran. "More Mysteries of Opium Revealed: 300 Years of Opiates." *Trends in Pharmacological Science* 21 (2000): 299–304.

Milne, R. W., R. L. Nation, and A. A. Somogyi. "The Disposition of Morphine and its 3- and 6-Glucuronide Metabolites in Humans and Animals, and the Importance of the Metabolites to the Pharmacological Effects of Morphine." *Drug Metabolism Reviews* 28 (1996): 345–472.

National Institute on Drug Abuse, National Institutes of Health, U.S. Department of Health and Human Services, *NIDA Info Facts: Heroin.* Bethesda, MD, 2005.

National Institute on Drug Abuse, National Institutes of Health, U.S. Department of Health and Human Services, *Research Report: Heroin Abuse and Addiction*, NIH Publication No. 00-4165. Bethesda, MD, 2000.

Olive, M. F. "Pain Killer Analogs." In Triggle, D. J. (ed.). *Designer Drugs*. Philadelphia: Chelsea House, 2004, pp. 72–82.

Schmitz, R. "Friedrich Wilhelm Serturner and the Discovery of Morphine." *Pharmacology History* 27 (1985): 61–74.

Snyder, S. H. and G. W. Pasternak. "Historical Review: Opioid Receptors." *Trends in Pharmcological Science* 24 (2003): 198–205.

Stein, C., M. Schafer, and H. Machelska. "Why is Morphine Not the Ultimate Analgesic and What Can be Done to Improve It?" *Journal of Pain* 1 (2000): 51–56.

Waldohoer, M., S. E. Bartlett, and J. L. Whistler. "Opioid Receptors." *Annual Review of Biochemistry* 73 (2004): 953–990.

Further Reading

Booth, M. *Opium: A History.* New York: St. Martin's Griffin, 1996.

de Quincy, Thomas. *Confessions of an English Opium Eater.* New York: J. T. Little and Ives, 1932.

Hodgson, B. *In the Arms of Morpheus: The Tragic History of Laudanum, Morphine, and Patent Medicines.* Buffalo, NY: Firefly Books, 2001.

Hodgson, B. *Opium: A Portrait of a Heavenly Demon.* San Francisco: Chronicle Books, 1999.

Julien, R. M. "Nonnarcotic, Anti-inflamatory Analgesics." In Julien, R. M. (ed.). *A Primer for Drug Action: A Concise Nontechnical Guide to the Actions, Uses, and Side Effects of Psychoactive Drugs,* 9th ed. New York: Worth Publishers, 2001, pp. 287–298.

Olive, M. F. "Pain Killer Analogs." In Triggle, D. J. (ed.). *Designer Drugs.* Philadelphia: Chelsea House, 2004, pp. 72–82.

Schmitz, R. "Friedrich Wilhelm Serturner and the Discovery of Morphine." *Pharmacology History* 27 (1985): 61–74.

http://www.ampainsoc.org

American Pain Society

Current issues and trends in pain research are discussed in detail. Provides general information about pain to the public.

http://www.painfoundation.org

American Pain Foundation

This website provides testimonials about the experiences of people in pain. Links are available to help people in pain, as well as those who are interested in different types of pain that occur in everyday life.

www.hosppract.com/issues/2000/07/brook.htm

"Chronic Pain: 1. A New Disease?" Hospital Practice

Provides information on the biological bases for pain within the human body.

www.Drugabuse.gov

National Institutes on Drug Abuse

An extensive website containing information for children and parents, teachers and students, and researchers and health professionals.

www.health.org

Prevention Online (PREVLINE)

U.S. Department of Health and Human Services and the Substance Abuse and Mental Health Services Administration (SAMHSA) national clearinghouse for alcohol and drug information. Provides information about prevention, treatment, and recovery.

www.unodc.org/unodc/index.html

United Nations Office of Drugs and Crime

Opium trends in production and distribution are discussed in detail.

www.dea.gov

U.S. Drug Enforcement Administration

Contains legal information about drug use and drug abuse.

Index

Index

Picture Credits

About the Author

Gregory D. Busse is an Assistant Professor in the Department of Psychology at George Washington University. Prior to this appointment, he was a Postdoctoral Fellow at the Medical University of South Carolina's Center for Drug and Alcohol Programs. Dr. Busse received his Bachelor's degree in psychology from Tulane University in New Orleans, Louisiana, and a Master's and Doctorate in psychology at American University in Washington, D.C. In 2003, Dr. Busse was named American University's Graduate Scholar of the Year. In 2004, he was awarded the Early Investigator Award from the College on Problems of Drug Dependence. His research focuses on the biological and behavioral bases of drug and alcohol addiction. He has published in numerous academic journals including *Progress in Neuro-psychopharmacology and Biological Psychiatry, Neurotoxicology and Teratology* and *Pharmacology, Biochemistry and Behavior.*

About the Editor

David J. Triggle is a University Professor and a Distinguished Professor in the School of Pharmacy and Pharmaceutical Sciences at the State University of New York at Buffalo. He studied in the United Kingdom and earned his B.Sc. degree in chemistry from the University of Southampton and a Ph.D. degree in chemistry at the University of Hull. Following postdoctoral work at the University of Ottawa in Canada and the University of London in the United Kingdom, he assumed a position at the School of Pharmacy at Buffalo. He served as Chairman of the Department of Biochemical Pharmacology from 1971 to 1985 and as Dean of the School of Pharmacy from 1985 to 1995. From 1995 to 2001 he served as the Dean of the Graduate School, and as the University Provost from 2000 to 2001. He is the author of several books dealing with the chemical pharmacology of the autonomic nervous system and drug-receptor interactions, some 400 scientific publications, and has delivered over 1,000 lectures worldwide on his research.